29
33
37
37

Prairie Laureate

The Collected Poems of
Robert Lee Brothers

Edited by
Susan Ford Wiltshire

with an afterword by
Barbara Jo Brothers

EAKIN PRESS ★ Austin, Texas

For all our fathers

FIRST EDITION

Copyright © 1998
By Robert Lee Brothers

Published in the United States of America
By Eakin Press
A Division of Sunbelt Media, Inc.
P.O. Box 90159
Austin, Texas 78709
email: eakinpub@sig.net

2 3 4 5 6 7 8 9

ISBN 1-57168-169-8

Library of Congress Cataloging -in-Publication Data

Brothers, Robert Lee, 1908-1979.
    Prairie Laureate: The Collected Poems of Robert Lee Brothers / edited by
Susan Ford Wiltshire : with an afterword by Barbara Jo Brothers.
        p.   cm.
    Includes bibliographical references and index.
    ISBN 1-57168-169-8
    1. Farm life--Texas--Poetry. 2. Nature--Poetry. I. Wiltshire, Susan Ford,
1941-   .
PS3503.R755A17 1998
811'.54--dc21   97-14511
                                                                        CIP

Contents

I
Democracy of Dust

Citizens of The Soil

Reflections and Shadows

Exiles From Eden

II
The Hidden Harp

Foreword, by
    Arthur M. Sampley 38

Of Nature . . .

. . . And Human Nature

III
Threescore and Ten

In Hemispheres of Need

Book of Day

With Every Spring That Passes

This Final Cleft

Epitaph to Other Days

IV
Late Harvest

vi

Editor's Introduction

Robert Lee Brothers (1908-1979) more than passed the test he set for himself in "Epilogue," the final poem of *The Hidden Harp* which won the Texas Institute of Letters Award for Poetry in 1953:

The stuff of which poems are made
Should never warp or rust or fade.
However fragile the design,
The mettled merit of each line
Should be assayed with care and wrought
To gracefully display the thought.

The poem that cannot endure
Neglect and dust was never pure
But tainted with the base alloys
That taste decries and time destroys.
Allow me, then, the darkest shelf
Whereon to take the test myself;
For if I fail myself, dear friend,
I fail you also to
THE END.

During his lifetime Brothers published two other collections of poetry. The first was *Democracy of Dust* (1947); the last was *Threescore and Ten* (1963). At the time of his death, he had compiled and arranged but not yet published a fourth collection, *Late Harvest*. All four collections are included in this volume.

Many of Brothers' poems were first published in a variety of small journals. His stature as a poet was attested during his lifetime not only by the Texas Institute of Letters award but also by the high regard accorded him by other poets, evidenced in the forewords to the three published volumes. These include Clement Wood (*Democracy of Dust*), Arthur M. Sampley (*The Hidden Harp*), and William D. Barney (*Threescore and Ten*). Wood writes, for example, "*Democracy of Dust* is the finest first volume of poetry I have every encountered in manuscript form—and I include my own among these. From start to finish, it glows with a perfection of finish we find elsewhere only in such masters as Edwin Arlington Robinson and A.E. Housman."

The great Italian writer Primo Levi, writing of his experiences in Auschwitz in *The Reawakening*, tells of a small child, the youngest of the camp, perhaps no more than three years old. The child belonged to nobody and had no name. He could not speak because no one had bothered to teach him. He had never seen a tree. The child died in the first days of March, 1945. "Nothing remains of him," writes Levi. "He bears witness through these words of mine."

In a similar way, the words of Robert Lee Brothers bear witness to lives that would otherwise be lost to us. Two poems in this volume, "A Little Boy Named Fred" and "Requiem for a Foundling," treat the deaths of small children whose passage on this earth would otherwise have left no trace. Not only these children but a whole village full of memorable characters become permanent for us because of these pages. Every time Brothers paints a verbal portrait—for example in "Names that Frame a Memory," "Requiem for Aunt Martha" and "Willie Dan"—those individuals rise to populate our own imaginative world. Brothers' more rakish characters, among them "Deacon Dulby," "Milly Malone," and the lawyer McPeavy in "Inquest," are at least equally memorable.

But Robert Lee Brothers is an acute student of physical

as well as human nature. Vanderbilt literary critic Vereen M. Bell compares Brothers with Robert Frost in this regard: "Brothers may use Emily Dickinson's verse forms but his mentality is Robert Frost's, Texas version, in that he sees everything human as being subjugated to and both diminished and enhanced by natural forces. Whatever else he is writing about on the surface, this seems to me to be the unsentimental undertow in all these poems." Bell adds that this way of relating to Texas and to nature is itself going out of the public domain, another reason for preserving the Brothers legacy in this volume.

Robert Lee Brothers combines an eye for the particular, a grasp of the whole, and a slantwise take on both. Although he speaks to all kinds of readers, I have noticed over the years that men especially respond to his poetry. Perhaps this is because Brothers is a credible son of Texas, grandson of traildrivers, a rancher himself, a man who knew the saddle and sidewinder as well as the sonnet. My own father, a farmer and rancher in the Texas Panhandle, was so impressed with Brothers' work that he wrote Louis Untermyer to interest him in including Brothers in one of his anthologies. When that did not occur, my father—a man of modest means but great love of words—personally underwrote the publication of *Threescore and Ten*.

I first heard of Robert Lee Brothers during a school holiday in 1961 when my classmate at the University of Texas in Austin, Barbara Jo Brothers, came to visit my home in Lubbock. As soon as I introduced her to my parents, my mother asked: "Are you the daughter of the poet?" and went to the bookshelf to bring our guest a book. The volume was *Democracy of Dust*, which bears an inscription by the poet to my grandmother dated April 16, 1948.

Novelist Rachel Maddux once taught a course in short fiction at a writer's conference. While her concern was about the process of writing, most of the questions put to her had to do with how to get published. "Don't worry about that," Maddux responded. "If you don't publish your story in your lifetime, your daughter will publish it, or your granddaughter." It is because of his daughters that Robert Lee Brothers's life work as a poet is now being published in one volume.

Nancy Kaye Brothers Paris of Gonzales carefully maintained the manuscript of *Late Harvest* with the sure knowledge that someday it would be published. In addition to a title page designed by his friend Harry Jackson, Robert Lee Brothers left with the manuscript the dedication he intended for the volume: "To my granddaughters, Azilea and Dawn Janise Paris."

Barbara Jo Brothers is a writer, editor, and social worker in New Orleans. Her beautifully-crafted memoir offers readers the rare privilege of seeing through a child's eyes the life of a gifted poet who is also a father.

Poets and artists are the tithe the rest of us pay to support the spirit of the human condition. They bear witness to the mysteries and whimsies of the lives we all lead and the world of nature around us but which we most often, in our hurry, fail to observe. These singers wrestle words into meaning on behalf of all the rest of us, giving us the where and wherewithal to see what was there all along.

The quiet, wry, infinitely wise voice of Robert Lee Brothers merits an enduring place in the literary legacy of Texas and the Southwest.

Susan Ford Wiltshire
Nashville, Tennessee

Democracy of Dust

The Kaleidograph Press
Dallas, Texas 1947

Democracy of Dust, by Robert Lee Brothers, is the finest first volume of poetry I have ever encountered in manuscript form—and I include my own among these. From start to finish, it glows with a perfection of finish we find elsewhere only in such masters as Edwin Arlington Robinson and A. E. Housman. The whole book is quotable, as witness this concluding quatrain of "Forces":

> Earth's wild, primeval purpose
> Ignores man's vain intents,
> And tramples mighty nations
> When moving continents.

This poet shifts from themes as vast as atomic power with ease, to note the tiniest facet of life, as in these four incomparable lines from the sonnet, "Southwest":

> A little wind panted over the sand
> And bellied down among the gnarled mesquite . . .
> At dawn the little wind awoke, and prowled
> The prairie with a cold, dry nose . . . and howled.

My chief reaction, on reading poem after poem, is "Oh, if only I had written that!" This applies to "Winter Night"; to "Windblown," whose every word is jewelled:

The wind is filled with cargoes,
Perfumes and gossamers;
And microscopic insects
Are vivid passengers.

The feathered seeds go swarming
on each erratic breeze,
To populate the gardens
With rustic refugees.

To perfection of word-choice, he here adds the intangible magic of evocation, a broadening of meaning by the figurative allusion at the end, that is unrivalled among living poets. Unlike the pessimism of Robinson and Housman, this poet's attitude is that *All's Right with the World*, which ends:

And the earth wheeled on its orbit
And purred around the sun.

In the second section, no poet but Chesterton could have written "Ad Valorem," from which the volume gets its title. Read it, and ponder its every word. The sensitive wisdom in "Besieged, The Leaking Faucet, Transmigration," and "Psyche to Milo Hanton," is memorable and enduring; and here, as often, we have a character vignette that no one else since Robinson could have achieved. Try, sometimes, to compress more into four lines than this opening of "The Strays":

We ran away together,
As free as antelope.
We fed a while on passion,
And starved a while on hope.

The final section, *Exiles from Eden*, if anything mounts above the two earlier ones. It is impossible to overpraise the perfection of "Young Couple," which must be read in its entirety; and this is as true of the magnificent tribute of "Parting of the Ways." For sheer wit, no living poet could better the ending of "Jezebel," immaculately immoral:

> Her silks and satins glittered
> Like sugar on a bun,
> Her eyes were like rye whiskey
> And the tropical sun.
> She danced upon tradition;
> Laughed at the circumspect,
> And drank a glass of poison
> For cause and effect.

The whole spirit that made Texas and the country it gems appears in "Ear Marks and Brands," where he says of his two grandfathers:

> But I would give a lot to know
> What we descendants would have done
> If they had been afraid or slow
> To back their judgments with a gun . . .

> When social climbers pry and press,
> I give them my best pedigree:
> My mammy's folks were LAZY S
> And pappy branded CIRCLE T.

The sharp social vision of "Summer Religion," with its two sonnets, "The Convert" and "The Evangelist," shows what a seer of the social farce we have here.

This Foreword may have stressed the incredible deft wit of this poet unduly, because it is so rare a quality among living singers, and so tonic. But never forget that soul-tugging emotions are phrased here as superbly. There are more than half a dozen poems here that bring tears into my eyes at every rereading, the concluding "Long Remember" high among them:

So quietly death moved in and out
We scarcely knew he was about
Until his presence had removed
The central being that we loved. . . .

Down by the oak and the empty swing
We broke our hearts remembering;
And watched with Spot, the lonesome pup,
The sun go down and sun come up.

The earth and all its people are the richer, for the
singing of Robert Lee Brothers. He emerges, even in this
first volume, as a major poet. His next volume will be await-
ed with the eager optimism with which we count on tomor-
row's sunrise. Go without meals for a day, if you must; but
don't fail to secure for yourself a copy of this incomparable
Democracy of Dust, and let it grow with in your soul.

—Bozenkill,
Clement Wood
Delanson, New York

Citizens of The Soil

Citizens of The Soil

The trees had leafed and fruited
As though the boughs would break.
They needed rain, but nature
Sent hailstones by mistake.

The farmers cursed the weather,
The housewives, more profound,
Gathered the fallen manna
Prematurely from the ground.

Southwest

All day the heated sky melted and dripped
In blurred horizons on the arid plain.
The gleaming sun sank to the hilt and ripped
Deep in the west leaving a crimson stain.
A little wind panted over the sand
And bellied down among the gnarled mesquite.
One pale star roosted high above the land,
And a thin moon reposed with claw tipped feet
Hooked on a distant hill. Aloof and proud,
With soft and silver plumage all unfurled,
It preened itself, and sailed behind a cloud,
Flashed out again, and dropped beyond the world.
At dawn the little wind awoke, and prowled
The prairie with a cold, dry nose . . . and howled.

Summer Storm

The cloud fleet dropped a thunderbolt
Upon a company of trees.
A fierce barrage of summer rain
Stung like a swarm of angry bees.

The shattered ranks of elm and oak
Lifted their tattered colors high,
And held the ground in grim platoons
Against the raider from the sky.

The battle waned. A mocking bird
Called to the stricken whippoorwills;
While savage echoes throbbed and died
Like cannonades in distant hills.

Scarlet Troubadour

A redbird drank with dainty sips
Out of a lily cup.
The dewdrops trickled down his throat
And songs came bubbling up.

He wet his whistle, chirped a note,
And then, as if on springs,
He bounced a tune into the air
And juggled it on wings.

Forces

The plunging streams go bridled
To pastures of the sea.
The docile land stands harnessed
By human mastery.

But the air is charged with tempests,
And molten mountains hide
Their wrath with snowy summits,
Aloof, and dignified.

Earth's wild, primeval purpose
Ignores man's vain intents,
And tramples mighty nations
When moving continents.

Rarity

The leaf was colored by the frost
And lacquered with thin ice;
The only leaf in all the wood
Displayed by nature twice.

It curled and crinkled in the wind
As if designed by a gnome.
And not a millionaire had means
Enough to take it home.

Raindrop

I wonder what a raindrop is?
I fancy with a smile
The drop that splashed me may have come
Out of the River Nile.

Perhaps it is atomic might,
Extremely scientific,
Caught in a net cast by the sun
Into the great Pacific.

The problem of analysis
Is left for you to settle;
I like it better where it fell
Upon a white plum petal.

Clemency

I know a troubled heaven pleads
With speech of silver rain
The case of little famished seeds
Imprisoned in the plain.

The earth is touched and growing soft.
From dungeons of the sod
A host of flowers spring aloft
And bloom their thanks to God.

Now It Is April

The mocking birds sing by the garden gate,
And the bluebonnets break the leafy mold.
April, you have given them faith to wait
In the starless dark and the bitter cold.

If a feathered breast can cherish a song,
And beauty slumber intact in a seed,
Perhaps I can balance life's right and wrong
With immortal thoughts for a mortal need.

The Hummingbird

Bright as a rainbow,
Light as a feather;
He and the flowers
Come with spring weather.

His bottle-green coat
And gay, crimson tie
Proclaim him the beau
Of garden and sky.

In his apartment
Down by the gate,
Mocking bird gossips
Visit his mate.

Bob White

Hear him bright and early
Whistling with happiness
When the sky is blushing
At the sun's first caress.

See his topknot bobbing
Down the old cattle path,
As he leads the covey
To the creek for a bath.

When the day is fading
Softly into the night,
Hear his mate keep calling;
Oh Bob, Oh Bob, Bob White!

Homeward creeps the hunter
Like a guilty cur,
Knowing well the reason
Bob White can't answer her.

Winter Night

The rain tiptoed along the roof
On little naked feet.
It went away, and came again
In silver shoes of sleet.

It slipped, and made a sliding sound
Like the scampering of leaves;
And caught, and held a frozen grip
In silence on the eaves.

Rain at Dawn

The thunder crashed against a hill
And shattered with an awful sound.
A fleet of clouds upset and spilled
Their shining cargoes on the ground.

The dry earth held a pond and caught
A pool of showers, mirror bright,
Blue with the glint of morning sky,
And purer than an April night.

I knelt, and cupped my hand and drank;
Such nectar, I can well believe,
Poured cool and sweet on Adam's thirst,
And sparkled on the lips of Eve.

Windblown

The wind is filled with cargoes,
Perfumes and gossamers;
And microscopic insects
Are vivid passengers.

The feathered seeds go swarming
On each erratic breeze
To populate the gardens
With rustic refugees.

April Fantasy

A knight in green and silver
From spring enchanted woods
Came galloping on thunder
Through misty solitudes.

His lance was tipped with lightning.
His colors streamed behind,
A tattered plume of rainbow
Arching against the wind.

Over the turquoise meadow,
The hill of jade, and on
To vanish with a sparkle
Into the sudden sun. . . .

Ah, chivalry of April!
The memory will stir
When dead leaves softly whisper
Green legends to the snow.

All's Right With The World

The sun, with slender fingers,
Reached down and stroked the world.
And every folded blossom
Ecstatically uncurled.

By chance, and not affection,
The miracle was done.
And the earth wheeled on its orbit
And purred around the sun.

Campaign in April

The stubborn snow withdrew itself
Into the nearest shade.
And here and there defeated grass
Unsheathed a bright new blade.

A wild plum put a banner out,
And waved it back and forth

In premature defiance at
White legions of the north.

And suddenly the north closed in
With cavalry of sleet;
The blades snapped, and the banner fell
Beneath those crystal feet.

The hooves of winter clattered by
Upon a vain pursuit,
While green rebellions smoldered in
The heart of every root.

The Vulture

He perches alone in a leafless tree
And gazes on objects unfit to see.
Death is the master of his destiny,
    And the gallows hill is his eyrie.
He follows the famine, the fire, the flood,
And washes his carrion down with blood.
His feather are reeking with filth and mud,
    And his cold eyes are bleak and dreary.

Repulsive bird, like a grim scout of hell,
He serves the devil and serves him well;
By his circling wings the killers can tell
    Where the trail of the quarry ended.
Eagles despise him. And the lesser things
That crouch in burrows, or fly on swift wings,
Avoid the foul place where he sits and swings
    On a dead limb barren and bended.

Dust

Wild rivulets, the hungry cubs of rain,
Tore at the turf, and gnawed the mountain's bones.
The jackal wind came howling from the plain
To feast. Slow maggot time consumed the stones
Through ages that no memory can span.
Only the gray and formless ghosts remain:
Dust . . . whose atoms hold the entity of man.

Reflections and Shadows

Ad Valorem

The builders and the dreamers rest
Beside the fools and knaves
In the democracy of dust
In their respective graves.

From close communion with the earth
Their lives are justified;
A few by grace of being born,
The rest by having died.

For Potential Poets

You, too, will squander golden thoughts among
Halfpenny words you might have left unsaid,
And find that art is flat upon the tongue
Whose palate craves the taste of coarser bread.
If you must write, then do it in this way:
A breath of scandal with a subtle touch.
It will not bring you fame, but it will pay,
Which is the thing that most desire so much.

If truth is what your talent would record,
Age well your words until they gather moss.
Submit them to the judgment of the Lord
Before they nail them with you on a cross.
    The world forgives the follies done in drink, ·
    But never yet a folly said in ink.

Besieged

The wise retire to meditate,
And close the door behind.
No citadel can boast a wall
Impregnable as the mind.

Care and temptation lay a siege
With force and crafty spies,
But wisdom in the sentry box
Anticipates surprise.

When sovereign truth arrives at last
Uncrowned, with raiment rent,
He is not halted by the guard
Upon the battlement.

Glimpse

The sunlight striking stone,
A shadow's grace;
Never the sight of tears,
Only the trace.

A glitter in the grass;
Beware the prize . . .
A jewel, dewdrop or
A serpent's eyes.

News

The tidings of victory or defeat,
Once borne by a runner with labored breath,
Was old before the bearer could repeat
The ancient paradox of life and death.

But now, the news is flashed around the sphere
Swifter than thought or tremors of a quake.
And people on the street unheeding hear
The scarlet epics greed and passion make.

The Strays

We ran away together,
As free as antelope.
We fed a while on passion,
And starved a while on hope.

We found green pastures withered,
And mountain trails too steep;
The fold has compensations
Freedom denies to sheep.

To One I Wronged

You are avenged without your knowing.
The sin is not upon your head.
The lash that cut was your quiet going;
My shame the words you left unsaid.

The past is vivid as an ember,
Jewel of fire in a ruined set.
And I am destined to remember
What you may happily forget.

Points Of View

I glanced into the face of life
One day as he rushed by.
I saw the price he paid to live,
And how he feared to die.

I looked upon the face of death.
His pallid lips were curled
As one who smiles at those who set
Such value on the world.

A Fireplace is a Friendly Place

A fireplace is a friendly place
When backlogs cast the glow
Of youth again on some lined face
Dreaming of long ago.

When visions dance with leaping flame
And fade with the last coal,
Love is a sweeter wine than fame
To cheer a lonely soul.

In the white years when we are old
And ready to retire,
I hope we have a hand to hold,
A place beside the fire.

Formal Affair

I do not remember much of what was said.
I only remember that we spoke,
And how the thought groped blindly in my head
To find a point for someone's "clever" joke.

From many forks I shyly chose the one
That observation marked for me as right.
And then, between the midnight and the sun,
We bowed and forced a smile and said . . . Goodnight.

The Subtle Ghost

The subtle ghost assumes no form
Conceptions indicate.
But in the heart's red corridor
It lies inanimate

Until the senses reproduce
By the alchemy of brain,
Familiar mediums that raise
The dormant ghost again.

It whispers through the sealed gray cell
Where mad impulses are;
And makes an exit unobserved,
But leaves the door ajar.

Guarded

Somewhere within a darkened thought
Lurks a murderous word,
Waiting a tongue to give it voice,
And ears that it might be heard.

The mind has unknown catacombs,
Abodes of lusts and hates;
Let silence wall the citadel,
And wisdom guard the gates.

Transmigration

Bridges burn behind us,
Cross roads loom near by.
Choose the right direction;
Travel until you die.

There is no returning
Once a bridge is crossed.
What you take is with you,
What you leave is lost.

Flesh and bone are fragile.
Faith should be consigned
From the weakened shoulders
To the vaulted mind.

Noble thoughts, like eagles,
Wind their way ahead
When the heart grows silent
And the brain is dead.

Traveler at Dusk

Cast your cool shadow on my soul,
And light a star.
All day I watched the wheel of heaven roll,
And traveled far.

Steeds of the four winds browse and tire.
I hear them stamp
Softly beyond the waning moon's pale fire
Where I encamp.

Of those who saw a distant flame
Flare and sink low,
Many will mark the route by which I came;
None where I go.

Psyche to Milo Hanton

Ah, comrade, I have played so small a part
In your existence that you never missed
My little light that flickered and went out
And left you in the darkness of the grave.

I was the sober moment between drinks
That drugged your wine with certain memories
Which cost you a month's wages to forget
An afternoon or, at the most, a night.

I was the telescope through which you looked,
But always from the wrong end to distort
The shapes of truths you dreaded most to see
Enlarged by conscience to the mental eye;
By glancing through the lenses thus reversed,
They looked inconsequential and far off.

I was the indecision, like a slap,
Between the invitation and the kiss,
That thwarted you and saved a pair of lips
The blister of a permanent regret.

I was the pity that you briefly felt
Once for a wounded dove that voiced a moan
And fluttered helpless in your hands before
You cursed the scarlet drip and wrung her neck.

I do not feel that justice is divine
If I must bear the blame and punishment
Because I could not bridle the brute flesh
Or reason with your cold, skeptical brain.

If dissolution back to dust is all
To be exacted of your mortal part,
Then why should I be held accountable
When you are washed by gentle summer rains?
I had as soon chance hell in any case
As be immortal in the likes of you.

Journey

When once I made a journey,
I told each town I passed
My unexpected pleasure
At seeing, first and last,
A new scene quite familiar,
A glimpse of spire and dome
Solid and unpretentious
As those I'd left at home.

I watched the reeling landscape,
As far as eyes could see,
Dissolve into the distance
And merge with memory.
A meadow, and a farm house,
A funny weather vane;
And lonely, lovely places
I may not pass again.

I turned the miles like pages,
With eagerness to scan
A text so rich in contents,
And so American.
I think if life's momentum
Ignored the schedule made.
We might arrive the better
For having been delayed.

The Leaking Faucet

Almost inaudible at first,
It mounted to intensity.
The repetition trickled on
Through hours of monotony.

In such a small thing as a drop
Of water all my thoughts were drowned,
And every raw nerve was exposed
By the incisions of the sound.

The Aliens

They splashed the crowd with color.
Their soft, exotic words
Escaped the common topics
And soared like brilliant birds.

Resentful, we appraised them
With envy and distrust;
Local discriminations
In the brotherhood of dust.

Peaks

We choose our peak and climb
Toward the crest.
But on the way we tire,
And pause for rest.

Climbers behind look up
To where we are,
A gulf of space below
The nearest star.

Street in Wartime

The old street was unchanged except for laughter.
Each silent house was lonely for the noise
Of free and eager feet and doors slammed after
The passages of happy highschool boys.

Some have returned with painful steps that falter
On stairways in an old familiar hall;
And only they can dedicate the altar
We build for those who will not come at all.

The Skull

Within this broken vault of thought
That marks a field of strife,
Was housed the motivating force
That made a human life.

Knowledge of ages blended here
And secreted the key
That opened doors to all that was,
And what is yet to be.

Herein the human and divine,
The agony and bliss,
Became a purpose that outgrew
So small a chrysalis.

Exiles From Eden

Young Couple

They have found an Eden
None but lovers know.
You and I were banished
From it long ago.

Brief enough their sojourn;
We can sit and wait
In the thorn tree's shadow
Just outside the gate.

They will come bewildered,
Unaware that this
Is the ancient exit
Used since Genesis.

Cuttings From a Rose

They moved again today. A wagon load
Of battered household goods was all they had
To show for many obligations owed
Through season after season, and each bad.

Another hillside field of fallow land,
Another leaky roof and walls as bare;
He has become too gross to understand
That she still has a pride to make her care.

They passed from sight around the river bend
To where and what only the future knows.
He neither left nor took away a friend.
She kept a cutting from the scarlet rose

That she had rooted many times before
By many doors that failure shut and barred;
A broken stem with beauty at the core
Groping for life in ground that is too hard.

Parting of The Ways

Today I clasped the hand that guided mine
When first I looped a rope or held the reins.
A brightness in the old man still can shine
Like warm sunrise across the frosty plains.

And I was very proud and happy that
He held to old tradition and old style;
The high topped boots, the vest,
                    and wide brimmed hat,
The slow, kind words and easy, friendly smile.

Ah Texas, you have traced your map upon
His face with rain and sun and dust and air,

And filled his eyes with vision clear as dawn,
And sprinkled your sudden snow storms in his hair.

You made him as tenacious as the grass
That holds the earth together with strong roots.
The storms of life will come and they will pass
And leave him still unshaken in his boots.

Oh Texas, never let your sons forget
Their fathers lived for freedom and for right.
They blazed new trails so far that heaven set
The north star in the window of the night.

He, with the look of Texas on his face,
The sound of Texas in his friendly drawl,
Will look long for a man to take his place,
And may be disappointed in us all.

We met with gladness, lingered at "goodbye,"
Each knowing that we might not meet again.
How tall he looked against the western sky
Through my tears and the cold, gray winter rain.

A Gentleman of The Town

From fifty years of cultivated ease
Barth had acquired the taste and common sense
To underestimate his prominence
And treat his vanity as a disease.

He did not squander and he did not hoard.
He chose his friends as women choose their hats.
And those he favored with informal chats
Were seldom well informed but never bored.

Fate had bequeathed him an illustrious name
To which there was but little he might add

That would not, by comparison, seem bad;
And so, he rested on ancestral fame.

When the depression came and stocks crashed down,
Barth landed in the wreckage with the rest;
Taking the job one offered him in jest,
He earned the admiration of the town.

His character was strengthened by distress.
He bore his grief and shared his daily bread,
And took life's blows upon an unbowed head,
And died at sixty broke and a success.

Trustees

Fat, bald men with their bellies in their laps
Sat around a table in straight backed chairs;
Feasted on a heritage and portioned the scraps
Into meager little morsels for the hungry heirs.

Fifty thousand acres gnawed away by ten per cent;
Five thousand head of cattle slaughtered by a pen;
A thirty room rock mansion offered for sale or rent
By a brilliant, bony lawyer with a death's head grin.

Much to be considered when a rich man dies,—
Pale fingers worm through the tissues of a will.
Fifty thousand acres reduced to pocket size,
And a dead man turning in his grave upon the hill.

The Traveler

We knew him as a lonely traveler
Who shared our humble hearth and simple fare,
And charmed us from the drudgery of care
With the finesse of a philosopher.

What unrest kept him moving through the land,
This man whose talents fit so many nooks,
The fields of labor or the realms of books,
Where skill of brawn and brain are in demand?

No dog would bark at him. And every child
Remembered him among the treasured things
That childhood gleans from daily happenings
When life is tender and the season mild.

Late was the hour when we said goodnight.
Early the farm house bustle in the dawn,—
And silence when we found that he had gone
Between the fading stars and coming light.

And even now when rain taps at the door
And lighted windows cast their yellow blurs
Upon the night, we hear the traveler's
Soft footsteps, each time fainter than before.

Waitress at Breakfast Time

With a brittle voice she hurls a quip
That penetrates the thickest skin,
And marks her score by the red stain
Of blushes where the point sank in.

She runs the gantlet of male eyes
That see no more of her than legs;
And many leers have leaped at her
To fall scrambled among the eggs.

The Bard of Shanty Town

I knew a poet once. His skin was black.
And all the clothes he had were on his back.

His stock of words was small, and so he bent
The weak ones in strong shapes, or would invent

A warm and earthy word, dew fresh and clear,
That sparkled into sound and charmed the ear.

He had a morning song, and one for noon.
The brooks and birds and bees were in the tune.

He never gave a thought to fame and art,
But drums of Africa beat in his heart.

I knew a poet once, black as the night,
Who coined golden words he could not write.

Reconciliation

We had a joint account in life. I drew
The greater part and spent it on my pride.
But I gained less than what I lost of you,
And that which tempted never satisfied.
I built a dam of laughter for my tears,
And feigned the pleasures I could rarely feel.
I had my moments, true, also my fears
That some unguarded truth might yet reveal
My self defeat. But you remained the same
While I was burning with a secret rage
Because you were absolved of any blame,
And only grew more lovely with your age.
    My dear, I love you better for the knack
    Which you employed to help me win you back.

Joe

Joe could clink his words around
With a shiny, silver sound.
Seemed he coined them on his tongue,
Making ancient phrases young.

With a gesture of his hand
He could make you understand
Just where emphasis was meant.
People called him eloquent.

No one knew what Shakespeare wrote,
Until the day we heard Joe quote
Hamlet over whiskey fizz.
Then we thought the words were his.

Money's made, he said, to spend.
So he borrowed from a friend,
Whom his eloquence impressed,
Cash enough to treat the rest.

Some have called him good, some bad.
But our village never had
Any one with half Joe's sense;
He lived and laughed at our expense.

Summer Religion
The Convert

In the white glow of the revival's heat,
He hears The Word and does not understand.
But the evangelist is learned and bland,
And the soprano beautiful and sweet.
And so, this teen-age sinner from the street,
Urged forward by the eloquent demand,
Walks up and takes the prophet's sweaty hand;
The first and final time those hands will meet.

Thoughts biological beneath the moon,
Inevitable and shameful to admit
As devil driven energy that hit
Two homeruns on a Sunday afternoon,
May justify themselves with conscience soon,
And make him no worse than a hypocrite.

The Evangelist

Consummate actor, living a live role,
With clear, keen eyes that can quickly appraise
The best of many tried and proven ways
Of winning a large church or one small soul . . .
On those who dance and drink, or swim and bowl,
There falls the wrathful eloquence and gaze
Of one whom God has called and mankind pays
To force the better doctrines on the whole.

Adept as any Arab with a tent,
His caravan is trained in moving fast.
And each oasis sighs when he has passed,
Wondering why he came and where he went.
Even the local saints relax at last,
Backslide to minor sins, and are content.

Jezebel

She was a lovely lady
From her slippers to her hat;
Immaculately immoral,
And alluring for that.

Her silks and satins glittered
Like sugar on a bun.
Her eyes were like rye whiskey
And the tropical sun.

She danced upon tradition;
Laughed at the circumspect,
And drank a glass of poison
For cause and effect.

Yellow Girl

She went to the picnic supper
That is held for the harvest crews
When the corn is pulled, and the hay is stacked,
And the cotton ginned, and the 'taters sacked,
And a girl can afford new shoes.

She looked about for her lover,
Her tall, strong lover in his store bought clothes;
A happy, sweating, grinning youth
With a dollar watch and a new gold tooth,
And a face as black as a crow's.

They danced all night to the music,
Held by the magic in a banjo's strings.
All year they had begged the sky for rain,
And wrestled the earth for lint and grain
With the faith of children and the zeal of kings.

They walked back home in the morning.
The low mist curled and the air was cold.
Her shoes were frayed, and the heels run over.
But what are shoes compared to a lover,
A husky lover with cotton unsold!

Octogenarian

It may have been the mountain air, but still,
His corn cob pipe was rank. The brook is sweet
With water undefiled; against his will

He drank it now and then and washed his feet
Before snow fell. His teeth were stained but sound,
No thanks to any brand of dental cream.
He wore red flannels all the year around,
Nor bothered much to change, so it would seem
Contrary to the books to say that he
Was typical of nature's mountaineers.
He had no learning but a memory
That chuckled over sins of eighty years.
　　To cultured minds his life seems rather shoddy,
　　But Lord, his soul was loath to leave his body!

Rolling Stone

Experience was all Joe had
With which to measure his success.
And he returned as he had left,
Alone, afoot and penniless.

The dogs barked, and the little boys
Ran out from play to watch him pass,
And say a few shy words, and sit
Beside him on the green park grass.

But they could only understand
As much of life as he had known
When he was young as they, and so,
He left them silent and alone.

They followed him down to the tracks.
And each boy's mind, could Joe but see,
Pictures him as he never was,
And always wanted most to be.

They watched him board a west-bound freight,
And thunder down the iron trail;
A Marco Polo, or a knight
Still searching for the Holy Grail.

Man in Repose

He dons a virtue with his robe,
And blows cigar smoke through his nose.
His sins are folded out of sight
For future use as are his clothes.

He tugs upon a chain of thought
Until he finds a broken link;
And, grateful for an interlude,
He turns and pours himself a drink.

Ear Marks and Brands

My grandpas both were pioneers
And brought the family fortunes in;
Grew quite respected through the years,
And died in bed like gentlemen.

But I would give a lot to know
What we descendants would have done
If they had been afraid or slow
To back their judgments with a gun.

They call us patrons of the arts,
And honor us with lunch and teas,
Because our grandpas, bless their hearts,
Strung bandits up on liveoak trees.

Their irons were hot, their loops were wide,
Their visions clear as Texas air.
And younger Texans point with pride
To famous brands their cattle wear.

When social climbers pry and press,
I give them my best pedigree:
My mammy's folks were LAZY S.
And pappy branded CIRCLE T.

First Day at School

I set my watch, and mother set
Our little daughter's curls.
And soon her figure blended in
Kaleidoscopes of girls.

A bell rang, and they scampered off.
We watched them out of sight;
And wore our wilted smiles back home
And kept them buckled tight.

Boy On a Hilltop

He melts horizons with a look,
And in his burning glance
The waters of the little brook
Flow seaward to romance.

The chimneys spiral up their smoke.
The morning mists arise
As oxen groan beneath the yoke
And teamsters heave their sighs.

The smoke is blown out in the sky,
Only the ash remains.
The magic touch of mist is dry
And salty on the plains.

The boy has turned from hills and streams
With a reluctant tread;
Who climbed to feast his soul on dreams
Descends for want of bread.

War and the Farmer Boy

"I shall come back some day," he said,
"Perhaps in time to harvest grain,
Before the sumac leaves turn red
And wild geese travel south again."

The wheat has made a bitter crust
Seasoned with salt of many tears.
The bright leaves wither in the dust,
And wild geese call to deafened ears.

Though lips that spoke are silent now,
Love made recordings of the words
On wind and rain and leafy bough,
And songs of migratory birds.

No Return

My long acquaintance with her stopped
One year at half past June.
The door of parting softly closed
And locked that afternoon.

A silent clock and a shuttered room. . . .
I kept the futile key
Hanging upon a silver cord
Inside my memory.

When later we met there by chance,
And tried for a brief time,
We failed to let the sunlight in,
Or get the clock to chime.

Fanatic

He drove his words like blunted nails
With the harsh hammer of his voice,
And blazed the trail to paradise
With lurid signboards of his choice.

"Detour." "Road Closed." "Hell Straight Ahead."
A toll gate on the brink of death . . .
Oh, Gentle Jew, how they have changed
The route you took from Nazareth.

Private Murphy

The Murphy boy returned from war
Without a medal on display;
A scarlet cough, and haunted eyes,
And half his breast bone shot away.
But what impressed the neighbors most
Was, that he had nothing to say.

Broad minds in narrow environments,
By reason must expand, or shrink
To fit the molds of lesser minds
And their capacities to think.
Murphy refused the compromise,
And plainly stated why in ink.

Though local pups had barked before,
Not one had the courage to bite.
And the majority, convinced
By lies and prejudice and spite,
Muzzled him for the minority
Who knew too well their pup was right.

When Murphy coughed his life away,
They laid him in a hero's tomb

With reams of cheap publicity,
And words and roses in full bloom.
But what impressed the neighbors most
Was, that there was scarcely standing room.

Illumination

He lighted just as suddenly
As darkened windows do;
And all the shabby furniture
Of his life was in view.

Distant observers called it fame,
But those at hand could see
He only held a candle stub
Of notoriety.

The Aristocrat

Grandmother wore a gentle smile,
And a fleecy shawl of lavender,
And served coffee impartially
To statesmen and the gardener.

Her charities were unannounced
At any social benefit;
But many ragged people called
To thank her for a gift, and sit

A little while in luxury,
Forgetful they were poorly dressed;
And each one felt, and rightly so,
At ease and welcome as her guest.

A grizzled millionaire observed
Her through a thatch of bushy brows,

Remembering a slender girl
Who whistled while she milked the cows . . .

A cowboy with a weathered face,
And hands calloused by bridle reins,
Squinted approval at the one
Woman he credited with brains . . .

Grandfather's portrait on the wall,
In soft colors and massive frame,
Smiled down upon the faithful wife
Who made a legend of his name.

Long Remember

Beneath his smile a pallor spread.
The smile faded, and he was dead.
A breeze sprang up, and in the dawn
A curtain stirred. The clock ticked on.

So quietly death moved in and out,
We scarcely knew he was about
Until his presence had removed
The central being that we loved.

We followed death in solemn train
Across a meadow through the rain,
And turned back at eternity
With fragments of a memory.

Down by the oak and the empty swing
We broke our hearts remembering;
And watched with Spot, the lonesome pup,
The sun go down and the sun come up.

The Hidden Harp

The Kaleidograph Press
Dallas, Texas 1952

A shrewd and penetrating observer of nature and men, Robert Lee Brothers compresses thought and feeling into his taut, incisive lines. *Democracy of Dust* established him as an authentic voice of the Southwest and *The Hidden Harp* will add to his stature.

—Arthur M. Sampley

Of Nature . . .

Lonely Rider

The wind is a lonely rider
Shifting with easy grace
In the saddle of distance
Upon the back of space.

Roaring across wild rivers
It leaps the sunset arc
And draws the rein of silence
To dismount in the dark.

In The Time of Ripening Corn

The wind clatters along the tasseled rows
With sounds like boys make on a picket fence
With sticks as they race by, then silence flows
Backward in a green tide sweet and immense.

The blond corn silks glimmering in the sun
Are freshly washed in dew and every strand
Is brushed with a clean wind. I reach for one
And the electric contact thrills my hand.

Black earth, green corn and arching aqua skies . . .
Oh, farmer boy, rejoice that you were born
Where freedom gives expanse for strength and size
To body and to soul, and where the corn

Matures in an harmonious accord
With men who love their neighbors and the Lord.

November Journal

Wild geese
Lay curved wings on distance
And fade softly to the south.

A russet poignancy
Flows through the veins
Of wrinkled leaves.

The crickets
Fold away their fiddles
And bow to silence.

Sparrows adjust ruffled feathers
To the first snow flake,
And take for granted
The charitable crumb.

The kettle on the kitchen stove
Sings a little steaming song
In a domestic key,
And the kitten in the corner
Purrs a rumpled accompaniment.

The wind
Rattles the windows
And tries the doors
And, finding no welcome here,
Prowls on
Whistling a northern tune.

A chill loneliness creeps in.
I must open a bundle of memories
And find a thought of you
To make me warm.

Resurrection

The glad reunion of the birds
Echoes from tree to tree.
The traffic of the ant resumes
An ancient industry.

The high, proud geese go chanting by,
And tiny creatures come
To dance together in the light
Or feast upon a crumb.

The world is wrapped in wonder
When resurrection shows
The warmth of an immortal smile
Between eternal snows.

Fawn In the Foothills

The dappled shadow in the dawn
Materialized into a fawn.
I looked again and it was gone.

The shadow melted into light
Where nothing was concealed from sight
But the swift secret of its flight.

The Chisos Mountains

Stone fingers
In the soft glove of distance
Reach for the sun.

They weave space and silence
On looms of time
And unwind spools of wind
To make a storm.

They hold the lightning's fork
Between knuckled crags
Smeared with the crushed colors
Of sunset.

Sublimation

Is there a secret sustenance in stone?
Are colors sealed in cells of common clay?
Does solitude distil a fragrance known
Only to winds that breathe it far away?

Consider the searching roots of desert plants
That find a way of life where most things die;
They sublimate a thorny circumstance
By opening bright blossoms to the sky.

The Norther

The wind swooped low among the trees
And blew an arctic kiss.
The last leaf curled a frozen lip
And answered with a hiss.

A schoolboy whistled and his breath
Warm as the air of June
Blew from his lips in smoky puffs
And frosted on the tune.

The old man dreamed beside the fire
The dreams of all old men.
He heard the wind go curving past
And felt the cold creep in.

Corn

The tall corn stands in formal rows
Like ladies in green linen clothes
With tasseled bonnets and silk bows.

Each stalk is graceful and at ease
With birds and bugs and honey bees
And every idle summer breeze.

What farmer's heart could be forlorn
When diamonds of dew adorn
The quiet elegance of corn!

Morning in Autumn

The blue-enameled surface of the day
Was fresh with morning and immaculate.
New-kindled fires crackled on hearth and grate,
And soft on the air the pungent wood-smoke lay
Unruffled by any wind, while far away
Crows lifted their raucous voices in debate
And hoisted skyward to investigate
Their neighbors and indulge in ribald play.

The veined and wrinkled leaves were palsied on
The boughs they lately gripped with a firm hold.
A pallor tinged the sun's face and foretold
That summer's beaming look would soon be gone
With late reluctant birds some austere dawn
When sap is thinned and trees shiver with cold.

Deer Hunt

Soft eyed and fleet the buck and doe
Came bounding lightly down the hill
To pools of shadow deep and still
Under the pensive trees.

Spellbound I watched them come and go,
These creatures I had meant to kill,
And stayed to see their hoof prints fill
With flying flakes of feathered snow
Spun on an icy breeze.

Sudden Guest

An unexpected presence
Half-seen and faintly heard;
A movement and an echo—,
It was a hummingbird.

The briefest contemplation,
A dainty pause for grace,
And he had drained the blossom
That warmed him out in space.

A little blur of brilliance,
A sensory effect
Recorded on the conscious
By waves of retrospect.

Measures

The estimate of inches
Computed by the snail
Gives distance definition
When swifter measures fail.

Autumnal

How quietly the summer goes
From every field and glade.
The flowers wrinkle overnight
And all the colors fade.

The latest bird folds up his songs
And leaves without applause;
How heavy hangs the silence
Where a little music was!

May Day

The daisies jostle in the wind
Along the bank of May,
Among the golden drifts of light
Where snow so lately lay.

The spider casts his silver net
In surfs of atmosphere
And makes it fast aboard a leaf
With ropes of gossamer.

The mocking bird's inaugural
To summer reaffirms
The faith in lyric principles
That justify the worms.

Watermelon Thumpers

We went straight to the heart of things, then,
In watermelon time, in the cool fields
At early morning.
We selected with care
Our choice among melons.
We lifted and weighed it
By the tug of young muscles.
We caressed its green symmetry
With grimy hands.
We thumped with practiced fingers,
Listening for the full sound of ripeness.
Kneeling in a ceremonial circle,
We broke the melon and ate of its heart.

We savored the sweet and airy taste
Of the red pulp's sunny texture,
And the sugary juice that dribbled
Between bright lips
Skilled in the spewing
Out of the bright black seed.

I have resigned my membership
With the back slappers;
The fellowship of drum beaters
Will see me no more.
I herewith make my plea for reinstatement
In the select and enchanted circle
Of watermelon thumpers.
Do they meet there still
In the cool fields,
In the remembered dews?
Could I find them, now, this late
In a waning season?

Being's Responsibility

The smallest bird performs his best
Though few may hear him sing.
The newest leaf is adequate
In forests wild with spring.

The shyest daisy in the field
Can modestly assume
Being's responsibility,
Capacity to bloom.

Distinguished most unto himself,
A man in his conceit
Rejects the privilege to serve
For power to compete.

On A Lonely Farm

Nothing ever happens
On a lonely farm
But the wild plum blossoms
White and sweet and warm,
Drifts of petaled fragrance
Where the wild bees swarm;

Nothing but the plover
And the whippoorwill,
Mist along the river,
Stars above the hill,
And the breathless silence
When the wind is still.

Nothing ever happens
Withered old lips say,
Just the silver moonlight
On the scented hay;
Ripe old lips keep their secret,
Smile, and turn away.

Spectator

Somewhere between the grass and sky
I heard a lonely plover cry.
A nighthawk circled swift and shrill
Above the shoulder of a hill.

The sun's red ball rolled out of bound
Beyond an ancient prairie mound.
I wrapped my thoughts and turned away,
The last spectator of the day.

. . . AND HUMAN NATURE

The Hidden Harp

We hanged our harps upon the willows . . .
. . . and they that wasted us required of us mirth, saying:
"Sing us one of the songs of Zion."
How shall we sing the Lord's song
In a strange land?

—Psalm 137

We hanged our harps on the willows
And left our homes behind
For we could carry only
Possessions of the mind.

They tried to break our spirits
And we bent them into bows
To loose the singing arrows
With which we struck our foes.

We fashioned from our heart-strings
A harp to fit the hand
And lifted up our voices
Far off in a strange land.

Deacon Dulby

When Deacon Dulby rumpled up this throat
To speak our voices ceased and every grin
Was tucked into the collar of a coat
Or turned downward and curled around a chin.
Ponderous words sagged on his vocal chords,
Barrels of meaning he adroitly swung
On the windlass of will, and with the Lord's
Strength and his own he rolled them from his tongue.

The hands of the old clock upon the wall
Fumbled the time and dropped it in despair
Before the Lord had mercy on us all
And let old Deacon Dulby pause for air.
If, on that day, Satan was put to rout,
Pursuit was brief; the saints were all worn out.

Sunday Dinner

The heavy servings, baked and fried and stewed,
Were garnished with resentments long repressed
That sometimes spilled when passed from guest to guest
Leaving a stain upon an interlude.
This was the time they came to pray and feud
And be together on a day of rest.
Although their clothes and manners were their best,
They often failed to fit an attitude.

The women eyed the stacks of greasy dishes.
The men retired to argue in the shade
And wait the deadline of a fallen sun.
Among the idle ifs and wilted wishes
The children stuffed and sticky fought and played
Until the old house groaned for everyone.

Chorus of Youth in Chaos

We are the double-edged weapons
Ready for tyranny's hand,
Shaped on the anvil of horror,
Stamped with a murderous brand;
Honed on the hard stone of hating
Down to a point keen as pain,
Bright as the tears of your sorrow,
Cold as the lips of the slain.

Names That Frame A Memory

These are the names I will cherish always
And carry as far as memory goes:
Grace with hair as red as a blaze
And a traffic of freckles on the bridge of her nose;

Peter with shoulders as square as a box
And an eagle look caged in his careless brown eyes;
And Earl who always had holes in his socks
And delightful assortments of delectable lies.

A mixture of April and Cherokee
Flowed rich and warm in the veins of Marie.
Her eyes were the color of the blue-gray haze
On remembered hills in the lost autumn days.

We parted early and we journeyed far
Until not one knows where the others are.
But they will remember, too, I know,
Wherever they are and wherever they go.

From White Oblivions of Snow

Grandmother said when she was old:
"I dread the coming of the cold."
I asked her why and I was told
Though I did not remember.

Now white oblivions of snow
Have buried friends I used to know
And cast a chill about the glow
Of firelight in December.

Grandmother said: "Though I be gone,
The spring will come and life go on.
Hope is the light of every dawn
And fruit is first a flower."

Now that I know a little more,
I'm thankful my grandmother bore
The seed of faith in her heart's core
For this my barren hour.

Medicine Show

The trim goatee and fancy vest
Have gone the way of the Wild West.
The villagers throughout the land
Still recollect his one-night stand
And how with a persuasive skill
He sold a cure for every ill.

The children stared in rapt belief
At Bloody Knife the Cheyenne chief
Who gave the secret of his clan
To Buckskin Joe the medicine man.
The blackest man of all black men
Made magic on the violin
Or plucked out of the banjo strings
The hearts of sentimental things.
Old people came to testify
For medicines they begged to buy,
And Buckskin Joe was forced to part
With precious wares by his kind heart.

Some of us can remember yet
How we would watch with real regret
The gaudy wagon slowly go
Out of our lives with Buckskin Joe
And Bloody Knife and Dandy Dan
The Alabama banjo man.

Old Buckskin gave a good clean show
Before the days of radio,
And made his welcome bright and warm

On many a far-flung ranch or farm.
Most people never thought to question
His subtle power of suggestion
As he supplied with equal ease
The remedy and the disease.
His diagnosis, I am sure,
Was fraudulent as was the cure;
But not a soul under the sun
Was harmed or healed by either one.

So Good

Kramp was so good his folks set him apart
And tried to spare him life's unpleasant things,
Financial stress and petty bickerings
That would disturb his tranquil mind and heart.
They helped him finish what they helped him start,
And so he flourished as a vine that clings
To the support of sturdy, common strings.
His cultivation was a studied art.

When death removed him from the neighborhood,
They made a local shrine of his good name,
And what they could not praise they did not blame
Although a fool provoked them with his mirth
Because he saw how obviously Kramp's good
Was never good for anything on earth.

Social Exhaustion

A cabin in his background,
A castle in his mind—
He ground himself in culture
Until he felt refined.

His attitude was winnowed,
His character was strained
Of all the vital essence
That once the chaff contained.

The Banker

His face was a familiar blank
Set in an element of awe
To those whose looks were angular
Recording little of what they saw.

Although he satisfied our needs,
He left us heavy wants to bear
And showed a granite unconcern
Like the old statue on the square.

To laggards he was whip and spur.
To plungers he was rein and bit.
He whittled our inaptitudes
And often made a square peg fit.

When he withdrew his total sum
To open a divine account,
His credit amplified us all
By individual amount.

A Grave in Boot Hill

No longer quick, forever still,
He lies forgotten in Boot Hill.
The symbol of his careless creed
Is the unstable tumbling weed.

On what mirages did he gaze
Across the deserts of his days,

Distorting in his narrow view
The false gods to whom he was true?

He moved in shadow, fell in flame
His fierce pride in the dust of shame,
And died unhonored and unsung,
Bewildered, bad and brave . . . and young.

Literary Tea

Our bright words rattled in the room
Like pennies in a blind man's cup.
And what we said and said at length
Failed to bring the deficit up.

The tea and poetry served to taste
Were sugar-sweet or lemon-tart,
And the diluted quantities
Had small effect on nerves or art.

Some of us came to be admired
Although in a reflected light,
And those who obviously were bored
Were busy keeping it from sight.

The phantom hands of Dickinson
Fluttered our pages, ill at ease,
And the sharp ghost of Wylie's laugh
Convulsed the curtains like a breeze.

The Old Town Clock

For many years the old town clock
High in the court house tower
Has been the keeper of the time
And speaker of the hour.

Historic moments come and pass
As do our griefs and pleasures.
The old town clock records them all
In sure and stately measures.

When sermons stray beyond the text,
The ears of saint and sinner
Are gladdened by the stroke of twelve
That calls the town to dinner.

The school boy weary of his desk
Watches the school room door
And rushes out to freedom
When the old town clock strikes four.

The farmer casts an anxious eye
Toward the court house dome
As if to beg a minute more
Before he hurries home.

The prisoner before the bar
Trembles and holds his breath;
A minute more might set him free
Or sentence him to death.

At six the clerks sigh with relief
And close the business places
And fold their public looks away
To wear their private faces.

Young lovers hear the midnight chime
And find excuse to tarry
On wasted time that they will work
So hard for when they marry.

More than a mechanism
Of springs and wheels and gears,
The clock is a recorder
And guardian of years.

It measures off eternity
With steady, humble hands
And breaks it into segments
Which a mortal understands.

Unconsciously we pause to hear
The old clock's throaty chime.
It knows our family secrets
But it only tells the time!

Wellington

There is a change in Wellington,
Just what it is we do not know;
It is a soft diffusive glow
Of a kind light for everyone.

Whatever darkness clouded him
Has cleared forever from his eyes
And we observed it with surprise
Although at first the light was dim.

Not even Wellington could tell,
Or would, how it all came about.
It is enough that he is out
From having served a term in hell.

Whatever god gave him parole
Should be considered seriously
By those whose awful piety
Would utterly condemn his soul.

Parting

When distance dimmed his features
And muted his goodbye,
The day collapsed between us
In empty folds of sky.

From prospect of reunion
We fashion as we can
Hope's little jeweled trinkets
That grace the life of man.

Possessed

Now she is dead. Why wring the futile tear
For one who was too often left behind
With, "Darling are you certain you don't mind?"
Or, "Only you would do so much my dear."
In times of trouble she would hover near
And earn our gratitude by being kind
While she wove clever knots in ties that bind
Their cruel comforts tighter every year.

She burrowed in our beings with a skill
That undermined thought in the secret brain
So that we felt our self-reliance drain
Away through subtle channels of her will.
Her tainted sweetness lingers with us still
Like wilted roses bitter in the rain.

Life Lines

Three times her name was in the news,
Brief clippings long since laid aside.
Ten lines in all record her birth,
Her marriage and the day she died.

My curiosity has searched
The past but she has left no signs
Of her existence anywhere
To fill the blanks between the lines.

She must have been a frugal soul,
A virtuous and tidy wife
To leave such spotless poverty
When she moved out of life.

Lost Lamb

There are degrees in heaven
I heard a preacher say.
If so, may I not enter
An unobtrusive way?

Is there some smaller portal
Where I might wait and see
The proper soul's adjustment
To immortality?

Will saints be then assembled
In pews that segregate
Common denominations
From those who designate

Themselves with chosen symbols
To sit with the elect
And look with an amazing grace
At those they don't expect?

Arriving late with laggards
And standing in the aisle
While wearing still a human look,
I might forget and smile

If star-encrusted deacons
Should make profound remarks
To stop in indignation
When someone's dogma barks.

I am a lost sheep, Master.
Abandon not the search;
Upon my way to heaven
I fell asleep in church!

Fallen Angel

Her hell was air-conditioned
With plumbing laid to plan,
And she had raised the devil
To the surface of her man.

Her thoughts were mental grindstones
That sharpened words like knives
To cut away the silence
He stretched between their lives.

To all tormented sisters
She had a tale to tell
Of how the fall had hurt her,
But why she never fell.

Birthday Reflection

Age is a fact in wrinkles
Made public on the face
Of an expiring option
Secured on surface grace.

Hospital

The linen whispers of the nurses' uniforms
Puckered the stillness of the midnight hush
As they answered a muffled bell's alarms
On footsteps soft as feathers touching plush.
A new life hailed existence with a cry
While one, older, dismissed it with a breath.
Pain is the first sensation; those who die
Find that immunity, at least, in death.
The gentle shadows at my bedside melt
And day comes suddenly in one sunburst.

In every nerve life makes its presence felt
As I lie in a pain-storm parched with thirst
And reeking with an antiseptic smell,
Wishing that I could die, and getting well.

To Emily Dickinson

"There is no frigate like a book . . ."
I boarded yours today,
Miraculous embarkation
For ports sunsets away;

A voyage in the eternal,
And so superbly done
I saw the gates of heaven
Were made like those at home.

Repudiation

Her words were proud and trained and clipped
So that she could, without delay,
Produce a suitable bouquet
For those less artfully equipped.

She sent her little mental sprays
Arranged to please the culture-blind
Who smiled and put them out of mind
To wilt among their yesterdays.

When art took more than she could give
Of talent that it could not use,
She found the courage to refuse
The parasite a place to live.

Through What Wild Centuries

Unheralded the victor came alone
From the dark wood and daemon-haunted glade.
Clutched in his hand there was a broken blade,
And in his flesh a wound that bared the bone.
His tightened lips throttled an inward groan
Of agony, and his proud plumes were frayed,
And scarlet spattered every step he made
Into the twilight where he passed unknown.

Glad sounds of life ring in the once dark wood,
And in the clearings dew-fresh gardens grow,
And children play gay games where long ago,
So legend says, an evil castle stood
Guarded by ogres . . . Ah, the tale is good
To tell by firelight on a night of snow.

San Antonio Sequence
Three Triolets
I

The lights of the old Menger glow
When night wears a star-sequined shawl.
Where time is still and roses grow
The lights of the old Menger glow
Softly upon the Alamo
That stands the stronger for its fall.
The lights of the old Menger glow
When night wears a star-sequined shawl.

II

I cross the threshold of the years
Into the quiet patio.
Before the evening star appears
I cross the threshold of the years
And glimpse through mist, or is it tears?
The dear dead faces I love so.
I cross the threshold of the years
Into the quiet patio.

III

My love, the years have drifted by
Swifter than wind, silent as snow.
While we have lingered, you and I,
My love, the years have drifted by.
How beautiful the evening sky!
But it is late and we must go.
My love, the years have drifted by
Swifter than wind, silent as snow.

Jacob's Ladder

Jacob began to dream when he was young
Of a strong ladder on which he might climb
Above the commonplace to the sublime,
And quit before he whittled the first rung
From hard reality, but still he clung
To idle wishes that became in time
Impossibilities. He passed the prime
Of life but he was active with his tongue.

Repeating his old story without stop
Of all the troubles drink had failed to drown,
He stumbled out of life one tragic day
Bitter because he failed to reach the top
And could not find upon the hard road down
A single turn into the easy way.

Wild Violets

Because Jim was a silent man and shy
He was belittled by the local swains
Who had far more to say than they had brains
To say it with. And that's the reason why
He won Marie, without seeming to try,
One afternoon while riding down lost lanes
That wound around old hills fresh from the rains
Of spring and lighted with a sunset sky.

By a mad, merry, nameless little creek
With wild wood violets along the brim
They paused a while, and since he could not speak,
He pressed those shy wild flowers in her hand
In such a way that she could understand
The gentle things they had to say for him.

The Mourners

The friends and neighbors gathered round
With bare, bowed heads before the mound
Of fresh-cut blooms and new-turned clay
That housed the dust of old man Gray.

The banker thought: "My hands are tied;
His note came due the day he died.
I hope and pray he was insured,
The loan was small but unsecured."

The preacher thought: "His flesh was weak,
His spirit moved by alcohol;
Oh, blessed are the pure and meek,
But old Gray was a prodigal."

The little boy: "Poor Mister Gray,
He took us fishing, taught us games,
He shared our secrets, knew own names,
We'll miss him now he's gone away."

His wife remembered his old marriage vow:
"With all my worldly goods I thee endow."
She shared with him a cheerful poverty,
Her sole inheritance and cheerless now.

The old dog thought: "My master's late.
I've watched and waited at the gate.
The wind grows cold, a star is falling.
The house is dark, no voice is calling."

The crowd soon scattered,
The roses shattered,
The iron gates were barred;
And moonrise found
A silent mound,
A lonely dog on guard.

Passenger

They pressed the ticket in his hand,
To where he did not know,
And traveled with him down the line
As far as parents go.

They left him at a darkened stop
To take a route unknown.
His destination was a blank
He had to fill alone.

Succumbing to acceptance then,
He put his fears aside
And rummaged through the luggage
They were thoughtful to provide.

He found a mind packed full of facts
He had not learned to use;
A conscience difficult to wear
And easy to abuse;

A belted pride that girded him
By one excessive notch;
A heart he consequently pawned
As often as his watch.

He still is changing trains of thought.
He is not one who drops
From sight to purchase permanence
In obscure whistle stops.

At many junctions here and there
We meet him now and then,
A little tired and travel-stained,
A trifle gray and thin.

Though traveled and experienced,
He has somehow contrived
To be aboard the latest train
That has not yet arrived.

Beyond The Deep and Dreamless Sleep
Mother's Day

Mother, what is there to say
On this designated day
That is not already said
To the living, for the dead?

Does it matter that the grass
Grows where people used to pass?
That the moss obliterates
Monumental names and dates?

In the earth where you repose
Time eliminates the rose
As it does the loved ones who
Planted roses here for you.

Now I watch, but soon I must
Sleep beside you with the dust
Still and dreamless on my eyes . . .
Wake me, Mother, when you rise.

Fulfillment

Life is like an empty bowl
Glazed without and bare within
When a man denies his soul
All that God has given men.

Vessels made of common clay,
Measured for capacity
Serve their purpose well if they
Fill their rounded symmetry.

Strange in the Sunset

Had I not returned,
The memory would still be folded
Intact and comforting
Among old possessions.

The familiar hills
Are indifferent to my changes,
And the birds and I no longer
Whistle the same tunes.

The little creek retiring
To a narrower bed
Covers itself with silence
And smooth sand.

In the church yard gaunt cedars
Shush me with leafy whispers.
Strange in the sunset, my shadow
Is the only ghost on the landscape.

Epilogue

The stuff of which poems are made
Should never warp or rust or fade.
However fragile the design,
The mettled merit of each line
Should be assayed with care and wrought
To gracefully display the thought.

The poem that cannot endure
Neglect and dust was never pure
But tainted with the base alloys
That taste decries and time destroys.
Allow me, then, the darkest shelf
Whereon to take the test myself;
For if I fail myself, dear friend,
I fail you also to
                    THE END

Threescore and Ten

The Naylor Company
San Antonio, Texas 1963

Three tests are what I ask of anyone who can be named a poet: he must love his language, he most love his land, he must love his people. He can be taught to arrange words in various queer ways, and he can learn to ape cynicism and sundry intellectual postures. This may help him secure a brief reputation. But without this threefold love nothing profits his trade as a Maker.

In Robert Lee Brothers the land has a rich and insufficiently appreciated voice. At times a wry sadness is in it, and here and there comes an admission of human failure. But the poems carry within them their own redemptive power. They are exquisitely tender where the foibles of men are concerned; they are passionately at one with their native scene; they are frequently afire with the just phrase, the lightning stroke of the inevitable word.

Occasionally a stanza will remind you, with its absolute compression and starkness of terms, of another rare lyricist, Emily Dickinson. But this is not to say the style derives from the Yankee poetess. This is masculine poetry, from a hand that has roped calves, bitted a bronc, turned a furrow. The comparison is useful only in a limited sense; it is a strange juxtaposition, the Yankee spinster, the Texas rancher. You think of it only to point marveling to the depth of sensibility and the adroit skill with words. Only a sharp and individual mind of its own can capture as much imagination, as much verbal joy, in so short a space as Robert Lee Brothers does

time and again. I think of "the wild bee goes about transla-
tions of the rose," "a pause of redbirds," "farther than
postage, farther than fare," "to stop with iron shuffle."

Love of the land shows in every seam of his poetry,
even though drouth and hostility in the soil have had a
hard part in the shaping of the man. Some of the harsher
poems, "Storm," "Desert-born," "Drouth-stricken" are
counterbalanced by a tenderness in others, "Spring
Statement," "Rain after Drouth," "Field in Winter."

I confess I am most taken with his portraits of men and
women of the Texas Hinterland, and for that matter, the
heart of the world itself. If rough tragic strokes are laid
down, they are more often than not relieved by slightly-
poking fun. Not the kind that delights in the snide and lev-
els to the sneer, but the kind that opens in affection. Robert
Lee Brothers has added many an arresting figure to the his-
toric gallery of creatures to be loved in spite of themselves.
I would not want to forget the tarnish on the silver wed-
ding; the lady who fled with nothing but her scandals on;
the civil marshal who smiled and died; the poor-devil hus-
bands who must listen to poetry expounded; to Lonesome,
who was hell with women and horses.

The sympathy and the technique are those of a mature
and rarely-gifted poet. What is lacking is only time, for I
have a conviction art so well-turned will not be permitted
to go into dust. Here is a quiet Texan with a voice that can
speak to sensitive ears anywhere. The best celebration of
his skill is not to leave him for afterward to sift out of our
obtuseness, but rather to acknowledge his accomplishment
now. I, for one, am grateful for it.

—William D. Barney

In Hemispheres of Need

Words

I have furnished a room in my mind
With comfortable words
Curved to the shape of my being.
Soft, soft is the touch
Of old association.

Some are no longer in fashion,
But the weave of endurance upholsters
The basic solid.

I have tried them
With the weight of my soul
And rested sustained on meaning.

*Dear Lady**

Dear lady, of whom no poet ever wrote,
Who never turned a poet out unread,
How can one reach you now down the remote
And dusty way we let you go unsaid?
The loveliest of views was from your eyes
Open to atmosphere both pure and kind,
Reflecting a heart-glow where the good and wise
Formed a distinguished circle in your mind.
The silver-service of your voice once lent
Distinction to the vintage of my rhyme.
I know now how unselfishly you spent

The bright and precious coinage of your time,
And how the will of your last breath was drawn
To leave us faith to come where you have gone.

                               * Mrs. Cora C. Ward

Poet

The life he wore was ready-made,
But it was he who did not fit.
Fortune never discovered him
Nor did he ever look for it.

Anonymously he lived and died
With only truth for an estate,
And fame exhumed a corpse to prove
The claim a century too late.

Period

I took a book with me to bed
And on the last page that I read
I found a little book worm, dead.

It makes me feel so insecure
To know a worm could not endure
The current taste of literature.

Synopsis

A lyric style is natural
As grapes upon the vine,
But taste was qualified the day
When ferment made the wine.

Two Profiles of a Single Poet
Pride

Expecting the attack without,
He stood prepared to win;
And yet could not himself control
The mutiny within.

Superfluous his brazen shield,
Although he clung to it
Until he fell among the ruins
Upon his sword of wit.

In justice we must praise his strength
As we deplore his flaws.
Could we advance the flag so far
Though wounded, as he was?

Humility

His summons from Divinity
Was briefly stated: "Come."
And the immortal estimate
Redeemed the mortal sum.

His talent was requited then
And he was blest indeed
By simple sharing of himself
In hemispheres of need.

Insight

When inspiration sweeps away the fear
That fogs the bleak depressions of the mind,
How brilliantly the guiding stars appear,
How clearly is direction then defined.
We struggle up the inclines thought by thought
To rest awhile upon some small plateau,
Only to find how little we have brought

Is worth the taking when we rise and go.
High-piled, the awesome thunderheads of doubt
Move in between us and the way we seek
That leads where light eternal shines about
The far and silent reaches of the Peak
Revealed in those rare moments, all too brief,
Wherein the vision verifies belief.

Open Mind

I opened up my darkened mind
By raising shades of doubt;
A tide of light came flowing in
And bat-like thoughts swarmed out.

A flock of hopes flew singing home
Like late-returning birds.
A poem burst from silences
And blossomed into words.

The Tragedy

I found him in a trunk and he was dead,
One hundred pages of him in fine print
Between the once-gay covers now the tint
And texture of a leaf that has been shed.
I roused a noted critic from his bed
And he informed me it was evident
That the deceased by an experiment
In writing verse had somehow lost his head.

Poor fellow, he had striven when no cause
Made it imperative that he should strive.
I buried him, my heart served for his stone,
And said a little prayer for all his flaws
And thanked the Lord that I remained alive,
Still capable of pardoning my own.

Book of Day

Book of Day

The day lies open like a book
For anyone at all to look
And, if he takes the time, to read
Some very lovely lines indeed.

The river writes a flowing hand
Across the pages of the land.
On margins of old ruined walls
Snails have signed their silver scrawls.

Flocks of wild geese flying free
Make moving lines of poetry
Which anyone can memorize
By simple scansion of the skies.

A wholesome hour may be spent
Reading the chipmunk's tiny print
Or learning how the wild bee goes
About translations of the rose.

Blue Frontier

Beyond the mountain's summit,
Beyond the range of eye
And man's imagination,
The blue frontier of sky
Looms silent and eternal
To challenge and defy.

The minds of men absorb it,
And they have made a chart
As intricate as intellect,

Uncertain as the heart,
And compassed by astronomy
For points from which to start.

The timing of a comet,
A star's geography
Are vast preliminaries
For novices like me
But I am a believer
And I shall wait—and see.

Summer Night

Fireflies
Punctuate the darkness
With periods of light.

A meteor's dash
Erases its meaning
From the sky's blackboard.

The sum of man's knowledge
Is not equal
To the quiet equation of stars.

Shadows

The transient shadows of summer clouds
Travel lightly over treeless places.

Flashing shears of sunlight
Alter a shadow to time's measure.

Shade is a custom of trees
But shadows of wings are whims of motion.

Petals of Light

Morning came and the flowering sun
Shed petals of light on everyone.
Streets were filled with the dazzling swirls
And bright-eyed boys and fresh-faced girls
Gathered them up and put them away
To wear in their hearts on a rainy day.

A tired old man in the city park
Folded them in the notes of a lark
And sprinkled them lightly
With splashes of tears
That hadn't been shed
For too many years.

Desert Born

The drouth that stripped the ranges bare
Left blossoms on the prickly pear.
The beauty in our land is born
Of stubborn root and cruel thorn.
Deep in their veiny fibres run
The burning passions of the sun
Together with the cooling flows
Of hoarded rains and melted snows.
Perhaps the root's hard way is turned
To deeper truths than we have learned,
And the sharp practice of the thorn
Protects its own, the desert-born.

Spring Statement

Tender is the curved touch of an April leaf
Upon the full measure of life;
Green currency of spring redeemable
In autumn gold.

The bees forecast no depression,
And there is no unemployment
In the industry of ants.

A minute is still worth sixty seconds
On the market of time,
And I have invested an hour
In white mystics of wild plum.

Drouth-Stricken

The wind fell suddenly on broken wings
With little flutters like a crippled bird
Leaving a feathered silence in its wake
And stains of red dust on the ruined grass.

Beneath the marquee of a blue-blank sky
A wayside straggle of wild flowers stood
Like weary dancers from some sad ballet
Passing from failure to oblivion.

The farmer thumbed through charts and almanacs
Planning a last defensive for his land
While futilely his wife tried to erase
The prophecy that dust wrote on her walls.

Rain After Drouth

The rain came softly in the night
In a dark hour of despair
Just after we turned out the light
And sought the comfort of a prayer.

In every blessed drop that fell
Was the reflection of a hope,
Of water in a long-dry well,
Of grass upon a barren slope.

All living things on earth then made
Some humble offering unsought;
Each root of grass a tender blade,
Each human mind a purer thought.

Leaves

The chronicles of cycles,
Stupendous odysseys
Of challenge, change and season,
And unsolved mysteries
In bright autumnal bindings
On display in the trees
Await wind's distribution.
Subscribers pay no cost;
Subscription is eternal
And no address is lost
Although identity be moved
To zones beyond the frost.

Field in Winter

The sun retired to a cloudy bed
And pulled the cover over its head.
Shadows uncoiled from a secret place
And the wind came up and slapped my face.

I didn't care if the weather was rude
Wrapped as I was in my solitude.
I wasn't angry and I wasn't meek
When I took the blow on my other cheek.

But the proud wind died on a note forlorn
Where the tall, stalked skeletons of corn
Stood leaning and listening, row after row,
To the quiet insistent whisper of snow.

The Outing

On the horizon crouched the cloud
Intensified but still.
Its color was a distant hue
With mottles like a hill.

My thoughts were playing airy games
On gentle downs of sky
When instinct with a cautious glance
Discerned the baleful eye.

We fled across a breathless place
We had not passed before
To take refuge in logic's house
And bar the futile door.

Midnight Walk

Our footprints wrinkle on the grass
Among the dead and disturbed leaves.
The circle of our silence weaves
Its own oblivion. We pass
A hedgerow filled with ruffled birds
Asleep, their heads beneath their wings.
We do not startle them, poor things,
By tossing random stones or words,
But leave them to their dreams of flight
And flutterings and churkled cries,
Where frost reflects a late moonrise
With stabs of crystal-pointed light.

Whirlwind

A whirlwind danced with dusty steps
Without apparent cause
To galleries of cottonwoods
That clattered in applause.

Growing with puffs of self-esteem
On distance too immense,
It tripped upon oblivion
In spirals of suspense.

Transiency

When spring returned the dead oak stood
Starkly pale in the greening wood,
The moss still clinging mournfully
In gray festoons of memory.
A pause of red birds was as brief
As roses sent in time of grief.
A hard-blown wind out of the west
Then laid the tree at length to rest.
A new growth rooted in decay,
And fresh wind blew another way.

Storm

The rumble deep in nature's throat
Is adequate alarm
For one who poaches her domain
On a defiant farm.

A claw of lightning slashes out
And sheaths itself in air
Before the brain records the stroke
That laid a forest bare.

The farmer ventures out at last
To watch the clearing weather,
And splice the broken ends of hope
And pull himself together.

After Rain

The darkest creature in the grass
Comes hesitant and slight
In tattered shadows of himself
To beg a mote of light.

With Every Spring That Passes

With Every Spring That Passes

My father was an honest man,
My father was forgiving,
And though today his hands are dust
The things they touched are living.

His well-thumbed books still read the same,
Each poem and each story,
And every sapling that he trimmed
Has reached a tree's full glory.

His pastures still renew themselves
From the sustaining grasses
That hold him closer to the earth
With every spring that passes.

Requiem For a Foundling

". . . and I named him Victor . . .
even if he dies he ought to have
a name . . . "
From the case files of a
Child welfare worker.

The earth will rock him gently,
Her dust upon his eyes;
The wind will croon above him
Softly where he lies.

The stars will watch him kindly;
While quiet ages pass
His narrow little cradle
With its coverlet of grass.

And he shall wake to Glory
Who never dreamed of shame,
A wisp from The Eternal
Ignited with a name.

Strangers on Earth

To say I know you would not be quite true,
And to assume I do would not be fair;
Our mutual measures can only compare
Those limitations obviously in view.
Old friend, it comforts me to look at you,
Your head still reminiscent of its hair
And leaning back against an easy chair
In bald defiance of what time can do.

I like the way your eyes can close the blind
To give my naked thoughts a pause to dress
And stand presentable in some conceit.
Although each tried to change the other's mind
And failed, we find the failure no distress
On that uncommon ground where friendships meet.

Last Train Out

Farther than postage, father than fare
My love on an unknown mission goes;
Her passport is stamped with many a prayer,
But does that make it valid? God only knows.

At the low-arched and lonely last station on earth
She passed through the customs and left us distraught
On this harshest extreme in the land of our birth
Where barriers raise at the terminal of thought.

Migration
Graduation—1960

The tender season fades, my birds have flown.
The nest has served its purpose and must be
No more circumference and boundary
Of those whose limits now shall be their own
As each migrates to some uncharted zone
And the full-feather of identity.
Had not the doves of Noah been set free
The olive branch might never have been known.

Let no warped thought turn or ill wind blow
Them backward from the high, uncertain course
To the remembered safety of a nest
That twig by twig is falling with the snow;
Spare them the bitter berries of remorse,
Sustain them in the hunger of the quest.

Poem for Patricia

Our moons may have a darker side than most,
But to the Vision Opposite in space
Be visible when light's reflected ghost

Is in eclipse on earth's astonished face.
We learned to walk with pebbles in our shoes
For reasons we shall be the last to know.
The pain was never ours to refuse
But to accept, and never let it show.
Oh God, Pat, I am glad that we are grown
And big enough to wash off our own dirt.
If we bruise easily, we heal alone;
It was the kiss upon the wound that hurt,
For well we know as long as mortals live
Their lips will promise more than love can give.

Little Town at the Turn

We have location and a name
That maps have failed to show.
But spring delivers flowers here
And gathers up the snow.

Change is a stranger on the street,
But distance is a friend
With space unbuttoned at the throat
And rolled-up sleeves of wind.

Bed Time for Barbara

Softly a petal from some tender bough
Of memory swirled down to lightly rest
An instant on the world of half-awake
And leave the faintest imprint of a smile.
The fringed closing of hazel eyes shut out
The countless lesser lights of lamps and stars
As tides of sleep moved over consciousness
That closed shell-like upon a pearl of dreams.

Proud Rider

I watch and wait with anxious pride
When Nancy takes her morning ride.
I see the dusty leagues unfurl
Behind the bay horse and blonde girl
As they go skimming fast and bright
Through shimmerings of boundless light.

The yellow rose of prickly pear
Unfolds upon the arid air.
The cruel, lacquered thorns are grown
With points set fleshward for the bone.
The armadillo makes his den
Just right for horse to step in.
The rattlesnake designs his coil
In deadly pattern on the soil.

When dark forebodings mount and roam,
My daughter and her horse come home
And I join in her happy laugh
Because Old Roan has found a calf.

For Two Girls in Their Teens

As you grow up and I grow older, dears,
Perhaps it seems at times a little strange
That the familiar undergoes a change
And form assumes new fashions through the years.

I think that Providence is very wise
To regulate our thoughts and visions so
Or I might seek in vain for Long Ago
And you might look too far for Paradise.

It is enough this miracle of Now
That plants the seed that bears Eternity.
It is enough that you have grown on me
As lovely blossoms grow upon a bough.

Sonnet to Susan

When first I heard my daughter speak of you
And saw your bright reflection in her eyes,
I chose the thought appropriate and drew
A portrait on the parchment of surmise.
Oh, it was lovely, yes, but when I met
The You behind the face and form and name
I knew such quality cannot be set
In lines or limitations of a frame.
My colors are too commonplace; I need
A glint of sunset on a swallow's wing,
The crush of cycles bursting in a seed;
Something superior to remembering,
For memory is album's occupation
With summary, and You are inspiration!

Train Time

I remember how I watched
At the village station,
And how the "local" came in brass-belled
With a tuft of steam at its whistle
To stop with an iron shuffle
And a long-drawn sigh of air brakes.

I remember the tensing of pistons
And the labored puffs of departure
And the blur of anonymous faces
Motionless behind moving windows,
And the rounded rhythm of wheels
Hammering away on distance . . .
And the flat construction
Of the ensuing silence.

Cotton Mouth

The little path that led to Kaye's big tank
Was worn to greasy smoothness by bare feet.
The air was torpid with the August heat
And green-lipped water foamed against the bank.
Over the depth to which a turtle sank
A bubble oozed and burst. Far-off and sweet
A red bird sang, and stealthy as deceit
The water roiled a moment and went blank.

The cork bobbed under and the line drew taut,
My backbone straightened and the cane pole bent;
I gave a mighty heave . . . and there it lay,
Its white mouth bloody where the hook had caught.
Nobody asked, but if they had I meant
To lie about the boy who got away.

Abner Creel

He had not changed. The faint vein in his throat
Throbbed purple and his little agate eyes
Skimmered about swifter than dragon flies
And settled for a moment on my coat.
"I see," he smirked, "You are in the same boat
In which you sank and that is no surprise,
As captain you could not do otherwise
Than go down with the loan that failed to float."

And I remembered then how once at school
When he had won my marbles and my top,
He threw them in a well and banged the lid
And jeered at me and cursed me for a fool
And dared me if I could to make him stop.
I tried. I couldn't. And I never did.

Young Lovers Late Returning

A drift of music on the summer air
And the diminishing footsteps of a passer-by
Punctuate a paragraph of waiting.

Suspense supplies material
For its own construction
While hope burns a frantic candle
In the open mind
At the fall of doubt's darkness.

A burst of late-returning laughter
Is a bright period
Ending an incoherent sentence.

Then, glancing at the page of probability
We see:
"To be continued."
After which we turn out the lights
And pray.

In Memory
(Miss Dot Lea)

I choose my words with tender care
But they can only bring
A fading sweetness to the air
Above the hills of spring.

To life she left her lovely things
So often shared before:
A faith that lifts, a heart that sings,
The little smile she wore.

This Final Cleft

This Final Cleft

When I had time to spend and the whole earth
Had all its precious wares upon display,
I bought the trivial beyond its worth
And thought that time was mine to throw away.
Forgive me, fellow-men, I did not know
I drew upon your strength and sweat and tears
And paid but little on the debt I owe
To those who gave their all throughout the years.
But what is done is done. The little left
I beg of you to take and somehow use
To help those my neglect may leave bereft
Of love and higher hopes and broader views.
I pray Thee Lord, oh, please do not refuse
My hold upon The Rock, this final cleft.

Offer No Help

Offer no help to the hurt leopard.
Let him lie in the jungle of his own thoughts
Licking invisible wounds
Inflicted by no one.

The shadows of famine
Darken the hollows of his flanks
And he worries the bones of wasted kills.

Be not sorry for this creature
Who is capable
Of sorrow for himself.
He will recover to purr
In his own environment.

Tarnish for a Silver Wedding

They cling together each depending on
Those qualities the other never had
To keep the mind from going quietly mad
In search of dreams that faded and are gone.
They keep the future constantly in pawn
For articles in fashion or in fad.
Hilarious, resentful, never glad
They drape their windows to keep back the dawn.

From all they never learned perhaps they teach
Better than most a hard but basic course
In immaturity that counts no cost
And would extend the grasp beyond the reach,
Retrieving without effort and by force
Those things which once were lovely and are lost.

Milly Malone

Milly was always looking high and low
For something lost and difficult to find;
Her heart at first, and later peace of mind,
Then faded flowers and the melted snow.
She argued that these things can never go
Beyond returning and she was resigned
To watch and wait and pity us the blind
Who wore our feelings where they did not show.

The winter came and proved that she was right.
The spring returned and proved that we were wrong.
And Milly smiled and lived on in her dream
Until reality touched her one night
And sent her plunging terrified headlong
To depths that closed in silence on her scream.

Lost Mine

Far from the last habitation,
Lost to the farthermost road
Is a ledge with a vein of silver
That leads to the mother lode.

Ask of the oldest prospector
And he will show you the chart
Drawn on the blank of a legend
With shards from a broken heart.

Develop the habit of hunger,
Accept the custom of thirst,
And thus be prepared for the better
When you have discovered the worst.

The Road

When young I walked a narrow road
To get somewhere, somehow.
What eager prints those first years made;
My steps are slower now.

Oh, I have danced for pleasure's sake
And I have trudged for hire,
But caution is a gait I learned
By tripping on desire.

Which mile was best or which was worst
Are passed beyond my knowing;
Nor can I tell which mile ahead
Will be the end of Going.

Haunted

Here, in a house built by plenty,
Arches the ancestral hall
Haunted by ghosts of people
Who never existed at all.

Flesh on a surplus of leisure
Spined with a synthetic pride
Rests on a polished tradition
Doors behind doors locked inside.

Mold is the medium of mushrooms.
Walls are frontiers to a mouse.
Shelter in which to change aspects
Explains every ghost in the house.

Summons the bottle-bound genie . . .
Magic derives from the wind;
Bacchus, a tragic illusion
Produced by a trick in the vine.

Centurion

This coin bears Caesar's image,
This land bears his decree;
I render unto Caesar
Those things required of me:

My blood to win his battles,
My strength to turn his mills,
My sweat to reap his harvests,
My talents for his tills.

On a mount I heard a sermon
That is shaking Caesar's throne.
It warms the cold heart in me
As sunlight warms a stone.

It gives old words new meaning
With points as sharp as grief
That probe the festered conscience
And give the soul relief.

What then for Thee, oh Master,
Unless humility
Perchance may have a value
That Caesar failed to see?

Sunday . . . The Bells Say . . .

Guitars are mute in Mexico,
The bulls at peace in Spain,
Around the world the people go
In pleasure and in pain.

They give one day to Deity
And keep six for their own;
How odd a thing it is to be
A worshipper alone.

No need to kneel, we only nod,
An informality
Between The One and Only God
And the one and only me.

Embezzle the Sun

". . . and follow the meanders of the stream . . . "
Oh, phrase of freshness, brief poetic glint
Contained in a dry legal instrument
Where contrast makes its simple beauty gleam
On old surveys whose designations seem
To fix the boundaries of lost content,
What moving hand by happy accident
Responded to a mind that paused to dream?

I like to think the weary clerk who wrote
The April words that dusty records show
Embezzled the sun of many a morning beam
And spent them on a little fishing boat
And made good his escape in time to go
"And follow the meanders of the stream."

The Long Way

I am grateful for the haze
On the distance of my days.
If I saw too far ahead
I might turn about in dread
From the vastness of a plain
Measurable alone by pain.
And, beyond it, there in time
Mountains I might fear to climb.

One step forward—one step more—
Foot behind and foot before;
Standing safely, holding fast,
With a point of danger passed;
Drawing in the living breath,
Breathing out the fear of death,
Balanced so precariously
On impossibility.

Conation

Perhaps the paths of snails may be
A wasted effort marked by slime,
But I, too, bear the shell of me
That hinders and protects my climb.

Through cycles of uncertainties
We blindly grope and slowly crawl

Up awful cracks in theories
Or fissures in a garden wall.

The Bell

The bell imprisoned in a tall, dark tower
Leaped up and tossed a note on the air.
It fluttered and faded and fell into silence
Like a lost letter or an unanswered prayer.

Inquest

McPeavy practiced law and other things
Beyond the point where most are honor bound.
He plucked on hearts and purse until the strings
Were harmonized in a rewarding sound.
His blend of elegance and eloquence
Concealed from taste the sickly tang of doubt.
Deception was the wall of his defense,
Constructed always with the smooth side out.
Whether they curse or praise him they confuse
Those issues which McPeavy clearly saw
Before he made the headlines in the news
By hanging from a loop-hole in the law
Through which he leaned so far he could not check
The slip that consequently broke his neck.

Compensation

Assurance, when we learn it,
Excels the gift of praise
That tarnished as we touched it
On undeserving days.

Genesis

When Adam drew the living breath
That made a mortal fact of clay
The birds of Eden sang all day,
Perched in the fruited tree of death.

Oh, guileless serpent, guiltless Eve,
Though Eden is a storied waste
The telling leaves a truthful taste
Too bitter to believe.

Ledger of Life

Faith is the seed,
Patience the plow,
Love is the planter;
The season is Now.

Drouth in the summer,
Flood in the fall;
Hope is the credit
Extended to all.

Epitaph to Other Days

The Probe

I used to dance on Sunday night
In drafty old farmhouses
With gay Czech girls who fit too tight
Inside their lacy blouses,
And people whispered, "It's a sight
The way that boy carouses!"

Those memories are wholesome now
As loaves of rye bread baking,
Or fresh-turned earth behind the plow,
Or sudden blossoms on a bough
Through which the spring is breaking.

I made a probe of conscience then
To pierce my heart and find the sin
That so concerned it.
But all I ever found was this:
That once I stooped and stole a kiss
And then returned it.

Uncle Billy

Though Uncle Billy never robbed a bank
Or even shot a man in self-defense,
There was a strong suspicion that he drank
Based on some circumstantial evidence.

Investigating further, gossip found
Some clues that seemed to justify the search:
His economic status was unsound
And he was not a member of a church.

Each fact was added up and added to
Until the plaintiffs had a righteous case.
The defense made objections but withdrew,
And Uncle Billy lost the sheriff's race.

He later died of an accepted ill
Which partially convinced the most devout;
But subsequent probation of his will
Left nothing but the benefit of doubt.

Muerte

I liked his reckless features
And took him for a drive,
But he stayed at the wreckage
And I went on alive
To travel in the future
Until he should arrive.

While walking with my children
Along a sunny street
I look into the shadows,
I listen for his feet,
For he is one acquaintance
I would not have them meet.

Ballad of the Avengers

The marshal wore a broadcloth suit
And two bone-handled Colts.
His eyes were blue as Texas skies
And charged with thunderbolts.

The parson dressed in rusty black
And wore a prophet's beard.
The worst he saw in any man
Was nothing that he feared.

The parson's words were burning brands,
The marshal's chips of ice,
And few who disagreed with them
Remained to do so twice.

The parson ranted out at men
And blessed or damned their souls.
The marshal kept a civil tongue
And shot them full of holes.

The marshal passed the Drovers' Bank
And reached the hitching rack
When two Winchesters cut him down
With bullets in the back.

The parson coming up the street
Soliciting for God
Stepped to a wagon near at hand
And slipped the endgate rod.

He smote about him right and left
Like Samson did of old.
He swept the lookout from his horse
And knocked the leader cold.

The bullets dusted his frock coat
And one that did not miss
Glanced off a rib and lodged within
The Book of Genesis.

The one remaining bandit left
As fast as he could ride.
The parson said, "____ ____ his soul!"
And the marshal smiled and died.

Lady of the House

When she invited Jesus as her guest,
She cleaned her house haphazardly of sin
And opened wide a smile and said, "Come in!
If you are weary I will give you rest."
Salvation not so easily possessed
Withheld Himself a hesitation then,
Could not be tempted in the way of men,
Nor could He fall, and He was not impressed.

The ancient lodger in a darkened room
Relaxed and made a wry, amusing face,
Knowing the landlady would keep in trust
His will that made her heiress to a doom
Peculiar to those of the human race
Who wear their souls out beating at the dust.

Sappho's Sons-In-Law

Unnoticed, unannounced and yet expected,
They come, these husbands from the busy streets,
To sit in silence on hard, upright seats
And wonder dumbly why they are selected
For such renewed ordeals as have affected
Their own positions in regard to Keats
And lesser poets who serve dainty treats
Not all of which are easily digested.

Each splashes through the puddles of applause,
And each shows the formidable restraint
Of unfired powder and untasted wine
Spilled by the grain and drop and all because
The trigger and the cork of just complaint
Snapped on a social defect in design.

The Ballad of the Lonesome

I shall tell you the story of Lonesome;
You may listen or not as you will.
He was born in a cabin near Peach Creek
And buried somewhere on Big Hill.*

He came according to nature
(although his advent wasn't planned)
To a family of ten on a homestead
Where post oaks covered the land.

He was weaned from the breast when a yearling
To a diet of bacon and beans,
But he never did outgrow the bottle
He learned to drink from in his teens.

He grew up high, wide and handsome
And rode up the Old Chisholm Trail.
He slept many a night by a campfire
And many a night in a jail.

He was hell with women and horses
And came home with two bays and a bride.
How often he bragged on the horses
After they and the woman had died.

They made him a deputy sheriff
By hitching his gun to a star.
He shot six men on suspicion
And drank twelve to death at the bar.

They shot him one night in an alley.
His life's blood seeped in the sand.
He tried to reach for his pistol
With a bottle clutched in his hand.

Now this is the story of Lonesome,
Of the joys and griefs in his life
Just as the hand of time wrote it
On the face of his second poor wife.

     * Big Hill—A Gonzales County locality—not to be
   confused with the general and legendary "Boot Hill."

Sheridan Heights

The weather-stained mansions on Sheridan Heights
Look down on the neighborly bungalows
In pastel prints and fresh-laundered whites
Fronting the street where the traffic flows.

They stand like barons of ancient estates;
Their gables are caped in magnolia leaves.
Iron deer rust by the iron gates
And brown bats roost in the scalloped eaves.

The prim gray ladies and the thin gray men
Peer from the past at progressive sights.
Many still knock but few are let in
The society of Sheridan Heights.

The Last Crusade

I came back from the last crusade
With a crippled horse and a broken blade
To a cold hearthstone and an unswept floor
And the good wife gone with a troubadour.

With a calloused heart and a missing hand
I made my way from the Holy Land
To my native soil and my native streams
And my empty bed and my troubled dreams.

Better the milk in a battered pail
Than a thirsty search for The Holy Grail;
Better the grapes from my withered vines
Than the poisoned cups of foreign wines;

Better the salt in home-made bread
Than heathen tears for the heathen dead;
Better that heathens live in sin
Than die at the hands of Christian men.

When opportunity came along
Knocking at doors and singing a song,
I might have seized him had I but stayed
At home in the time of the last crusade.

A Tale of the Middle Ages

The gallant knight, Sir Lostalot,
Came riding down from Likelynot
To find the wizard in whose spell
Languished his lady, Nevatell.

The fateful day they were to wed
His lovely lady up and fled,
And all they knew was she had gone
With nothing but her scandals on.

He rode his good steed Asinine
To the Shut Inn and called for wine;
And so befuddled rode away
The while his love hid in the hay.

How fortunate that he made haste
And she grew tired of being chaste.
For so he found her at the last
Between the future and the past.

Then rightly he redressed her wrong
As she expected all along.
And taking thus so much for granted,
The lady soon was disenchanted.

I would this tale did end with laughter
Of happy living ever after
As moral people think it might
Had she not stayed and spent the Knight.

Say This of Me

Say this of me: Here lies a man who tried
And failed and was still trying at the last
When time was called and the spectators passed
To go their ways about the countryside.

His tattered cloak of prejudice and pride
Measured and cut for fools was lately cast
Away for reason's fabric which held fast
And graced his being even as it died.

He dreamed of wings and was destined to crawl
A little while on an allotted span
Where roses are potential in each clod.
And who can say but what a rose might fall
On one who owed much to his fellowman
And left the debt half-paid in trust with God?

Late Harvest

Late Harvest

The seeds of thought that I have sown
Were mixed and hidden in the tares;
The precious few, now fully blown,
Are scattered in a field of cares.

The harvest is both small and late,
But there is time to pause and laugh
While sweating here to separate
So little grain from so much chaff.

Circle of the Hawk

Between the peaks of Yes and No
The hawks of fear hunt to and fro
For indecisions crouched below.

Of poor perspective, almost blind,
The little indecisions find
No surface refuge on the mind.

A silent sweep, a strangled cry . . .
No sign of one brief-struggled try
On unbent grass beneath the sky;

But on each grim, opposing hill
Are stains where some courageous will
Defied the hawks for good or ill.

Crux

Volumes of fact that contradict,
Construct and misconstrue,
Are valueless without the line
That holds the single clue
To truth we dared to try and tell
In limits that we knew.

Dead Wasp on a Window Sill

In broken armor still encased,
His helmet polished bitter-bright,
He glows with amber cruelties
In the harsh scrutiny of light.

Perhaps with futile sword half-drawn
He watched the sun all golden pass,
And tortured by transparency
Died solid on the magic glass.

Durango

The bells rang in Durango,
And little doves came down
To mingle on the plaza
With people of the town.

The twilight filled with music,
And we were very gay
Among the passing people
Where only time could stay.

Now, looking back through distance,
I feel the subtle spell
Of sunlight and the shadows
Around the old hotel.

A breeze came from the mountains
Where lately you and I
Had stepped aside politely
And let Tomorrow by.

Pobrecita

There was a girl in Lola's Place.
She smelled of shucks and woodsmoke
and sweat and honeysuckle.
In her horse-mane hair was a red rose
and in her mind louse-gray thoughts.
She tried soaking her brain in tequila,
having no better remedy.
Around her neck was a little gold cross
and the Catholic Church.
She died in a bordello in San Antonio
before the Protestants could save her.

Abuela

An erosion of wrinkles
and dark hair white-threaded;
blue tributary veins
sluggish in dry reaches of hands;

laughter is a silver bell
corroded with silence
in the mind's belfry
where huddle the memories
softly cooing.

Through cloud cataract
the vision's twilight
lingers over beloved ordinaries:
earthenware pots, a gourd dipper,
red geraniums in tomato cans,
and dry chilis suspended
from thatched remada.

A sigh that was once a song
swirls lightly the smoke
from her shuck cigarette.

Requiem for Aunt Martha
1861-1963

Positive her hand upon me
When I issued from the womb,
And her spirit still gives comfort
Though we laid her in the tomb.

Whirlwind among the cornstalks,
Thunder beyond the hill . . .
The field seems mighty empty
Since the grain has gone to mill.

I hear the wagons rumble
As that gin whistle blows.
Dear Lord, my sack drags heavy
On these unfinished rows.
Sunflowers waving in the wind
Turn where the sunshine goes.

I have two feelings in my heart
Like none I ever knew;
The lonesome one is for myself,
The happy one for you.

South

Lieutenant Colonel Silas Storm,
Still mounted and in uniform,
Stands guard upon the village square.
But there are pigeons in his hair.

The air and bus and railroad lines
Are formed now over Seven Pines.
By Shiloh Church the trucks parade
Where once was heard the cannonade.

So many things are reconstructed
And future-planned and misconducted
That anything out of the past
Is mighty good if it can last.

Lieutenant Colonel Silas Storm,
Still mounted and in uniform,
Stands guard upon the village square
In spite of pigeons in his hair;
And, passing, I salute him there.

A Little Boy Named Fred

There was a little boy named Fred.
He was born in a shack on an iron bed.
His skin was the color of ginger bread.

He died when five of fever and chills
and mouldy bacon and store-bought pills
Complicated by social ills.

That is all there is to be said
Of a little boy whose name was Fred,
So briefly alive . . . and so long dead.

Cycle of a Poem

Just when the thought was planted
Or how, nobody knew.
The subterranean process
Reveals no surface clue.

The soil itself seemed arid.
The promise in the sprout
Was pale in the prospectus
Tentatively put out.

In thorny circumstances,
Exposed to lonely skies,
The bloom in revelation
Achieves its own surprise.

Wayfarer

"Traveler, where are you going?
The sun is low in the west."

"To wherever the wind now blowing
Goes in the dark to find rest."

"When will you be returning
Along the faint trace of your track?"

"The bridges behind me are burning
And the roads are all closed that lead back."

Speak to Me, O Heart

My soul is sick of dingy thoughts
And clever images that weave
Illusions. Speak to me, O heart,

My brain so often is naive,
Inviting those incredibles
It later blushes to receive.

Miniature

He walks in golden silences
Along his own frontiers,
Attended by a pride of lions
He reared from little fears.

The Quirt

An old Comanche in Oklahoma
around eighteen ninety eight, give or take a year or two, was
friendly with my father and plaited and gave him the quirt
hanging there on the wall. I guess he didn't have much else
        to do,
being on a reservation and all and feeling a hurt
worse than an arrow or bullet can inflict on a man;
like living on after losing a way of life in one generation.
In a way I can understand, or would like to think I can,
how that old man felt, sitting there in the ruin of his nation.
Whenever I take the quirt with its finely plaited rawhide
        strands,
I touch something more than just the craft of well-worked
        leather;
I feel the Great Spirit that moved the old man's hands
to pick up the loose ends of life and pull himself together.

"And There Shall Be Wars and Rumors of Wars"

Old soldiers back from ancient wars
Would retell stories often told
Of gallant charges on the field

And thinning lines that dared to hold;
But those were times when hearts were hot,
And these are times when minds are cold.

Few soldiers now returning speak,
Though politicians quote the text
Of good intentions, unfulfilled,
For people weary and perplexed
Who watch survivors from one war
Meet children going to the next.

Reverie

This much I shall return unto the land:
The dust of dreams I dreamed when I was young
And felt the sun of life warm in my hand
And heard the haunting song wild winds have sung.

What may appear to vision as The End
Is but the limit of this human sight
Beyond which all the stars of faith attend
Those travelers who journey into night.

When in the quiet interim I lie,
All moral things aside, needed no more,
Wrap me in prayer and face me to the sky
And go with love, and gently close the door.

Thistledown

A wild sap flows in thistles
Bearing a Gipsy strain
That sends them forth to wander
The meadowland and lane,
And prickle the decorum
Of cultivated grain.

A vase entombs the roses
At shatterings of day,
And violets are passive
In fadings of decay,
But thistles are transfigured
And wind bears them away.

Bona Fides

The good things and the lovely,
The bad things and the vain
Will come to pass in season
And come to pass again.

Change is a constant factor
Of universal scope
Directed by eternals
Of Love and Faith and Hope.

Who toils for something better,
In peace can take his rest
If in his imperfection
He tried and did his best.

Rain in July

The first experimental drop
Made a little sizzled hop
When at first its tiny feet
Touched the paved and burning street.

Then on housetops and on trees
Raindrops swarmed like silver bees
Winged with wind, and everywhere
Made honey freshness in the air.

Noses pressed to window pane
Children watched the magic rain,
Saw the shower glint and pass
Leaving diamonds in the grass.

Snake in the Grass

Within my reach and just beyond
A four-year-old's experience,
The coral snake in rippled length
Flowed through the pickets of the fence.

In silent awe I watched him glide
By ten bare toes, and saw him pass,
A rainbow strand that disappeared
Into the shadows in the grass.

How natural it must have been
To serpent and to boy alike,
A moment innocent of fear
In which there was no need to strike.

Just a Few Words

Danger is a wild word
With the balanced feel
Of a hunting knife
Of tempered steel.

Dance is a gay word,
Small and neat
Like silver slippers
On a woman's feet.

Lustrous and ruddy
Is the word merry,

Like a green bush
With a red berry.

Like a bell tolling
Is the sad tone
Of the word Lonely
I wish I'd never known.

A Fall on the Stairs

Though time has honored him with high degrees
As he has honored time within his span,
He slipped upon the stairs and bruised his knees
And raised a hand for help like any man.
The fools who laugh to see the mighty fall
Will make themselves the more ridiculous;
What threw the old professor in a sprawl
May wait upon another step for us.
He soon was on his feet, retrieved his hat
And what was left of glasses dashed to bits;
Restored his sense of humor with a pat,
Thereby regaining dignity and wits,
And went on better balanced than before
He took the hand that helped him from the floor.

Man on the Street

I did not even turn to see
The sad procession filing by
Along the way to Calvary
Where men condemned must go to die;
What had it all to do with me
That I should pause and wonder why?

When rumor spread as rumors do,
And every judge and priest in whom
I trusted scorned such rumor too

(that one had risen from a tomb)
As superstitious and untrue,
Why should I not then so presume?

But still, I think that something strange
May well have happened there that day,
Else why do doubts so disarrange
My patterned thoughts and make them sway
Like vines entangled in the change
Of having old supports give way?

What's in a Name
(Huguenot Churchyard, Charleston, South Carolina)

The bells that tolled her out of time
Nearby the little churchyard chime
Where it is given to a stone
To bear the name that was her own.

But even so, it charms the eye
Of an observant passer-by
And conjures thoughts as gaily fresh
As doubtless she was in the flesh.

To mind attuned a thought occurs
As if somehow it came from hers,
An inward something from without
That bears no benefit of doubt.

The name of Barbary Bocquette
Invokes a subtle magic yet
For those who know a little more
Of spirit than the flesh it wore.

Old

To feel the senses failing
Is an emphatic strain;
Old eyes caress blurred faces
They may not see again.

If the hand that trembles
Seems grasping overmuch,
It is the wrinkled instinct
Foretelling final touch.

Even the shattered roses
Are welcome in a room
For the remembered fragrance
Of when they were in bloom.

The tongue grows repetitious
In trying to define
The thirst in empty glasses
Where sparkled once the wine.

To ears approaching silence
All words become profound,
But less for definition
Than comfort in their sound.

Vacancy

To see the shutters of a new house drawn
Is sadder than an old house in decay
Where life and love have both fulfilled their day
To some appointed end, and moving on
Have left a final sweetness in the dawn
Which time's slow friction cannot wear away
While there are memories to cling and stay
Like roses on an old, abandoned lawn.

But oh, the pity of a mortal woe
That lies like dust on surfaces yet new
And touched so fleetingly by loving hands
That lost their grip on life and let things go
Haphazardly to ruin the way things do
For reasons no one fully understands.

Vacant House

Unsightly on a seemly spot,
A blemish on our civic pride,
The house reveals in outward rot
What paint and prestige kept inside.

We pass its doors on cautious feet
Or take another way about,
Embarrassed in ourselves to meet
The truth that may be coming out.

Resentment

Uneasy as the atmosphere
In making of a storm,
The pressured mind intensifies
As the emotions to form.

The bristled nerves expand themselves
Until the attitude
Is indirectly accurate
To vagaries of mood.

A devastating flash of wit
Intentionally designed
Strikes through the insulated roof
Of an opposing mind.

Time Reports — 1863-1963

Beating the saddle pommel with clenched hands,
a gray man in muddy boots
rode back from Gettysburg.

A bullet fired in Ford's Theater
lodged in compassion
and obstructed the South.

A man with yellow hair and red thoughts
cast troopers before Sioux
and was himself impaled on The Little Big Horn.

A battleship blew up off Cuba
and sank into the past,
leaving a breach in the future.

The Armistice was signed
And Johnny came marching home
to prohibition.

An old man returned from Munich
waving a piece of paper
and an umbrella.

A paper hanger and his mistress
died under a mural of six million Jew corpses,
and Hiroshima became a Christian decision.

A bullet fired in Dallas, Texas,
passed through a president
and wounded a nation of guilty bystanders.

Among the fall of hysteria blossoms
children shout at play:
Bang! Bang! You're DEAD!

Ballad in Blue

Oh, had I been a working man
And bought my love red shoes,
She could have danced in any town
Her fancy cared to choose.

But I was not a working man,
And my love's feet went bare;
And oh, they bled to follow me
Down stony paths of care.

Then I became a singing man,
and oh, my dear, my dear . . .
How sad a thing it is to sing
Too late for you to hear.

Him

Our agony at utmost
Holds but an instant sway,
Or consciousness would crumble
And meaning fall away.

His eye is on the sparrow,
His hand controls the quake;
Or so survivors tell us
Who trembled for His sake.

Beginning is His Secret,
And End its consequence;
Imagination staggers
To bear its own suspense.

Rephrase the Ancient Question,
Articulate the Cry,
And hear the cosmic echo
Of Self making reply.

Dim, distant and discordant,
Down crumbled ages roll
The muted old confusions
We croon unto the soul.

If Silence is the answer
Our questions are absurd,
Redundant to the Premise
On which was coined The Word.

Time Piece

The old watch ticks and tells the time
A little slower day by day
And of itself will soon run down
To be put quietly away.

Although its mechanism, flawed,
May well be worn beyond repair,
Time has its own adjustables
Of which we now are unaware.

At last the moving hands must stop
Upon the second that will show
As much of time as we can tell
Of it from little that we know.

Looking Back

The good days were—but they were not
As youth might on departure see,
Or age behold in looking back
Through a mirage of memory.

There still is the Forbidden Tree
We dared not climb; and on us all
The pallor of that shady wait
Beneath it for the fruit to fall.

Willie Dan

Willie Dan was a laughing man
And over six feet tall.
He hung his hat on a deer horn rack
By the doorway in the hall.

He liked his jokes and whiskey straight
And tales of the Texas Trail.
He could judge the weight of a Texas steer
As close as a stock yard scale.

He wore high boots and silver spurs.
His horse had an easy pace.
He wore a vest and a watch and chain
And a big smile on his face.

There wasn't a man or woman or child,
A house cat or a coon hound pup
Who didn't light with a welcome sign
When old Willie Dan rode up.
Then he rode on to the Far Away
Where the trails are distant and dim,
But the folks and country he loved so much
Still love and remember him.

Old Folks at Home

Keep them clean and quiet,
Speak to one and all
Tritely as the mottoes
Cheapening the wall.

Feel the failing pulses,
Wipe the clotted nose,
Give the hypodermic's
Dubious repose.

Heed no curse or blessing,
But should you hear one say:
"I forgive your kindness,"
Kneel by his bed and pray.

The Word

When I was a little boy
Living in the South,
I found a tangy word one day
And popped it in my mouth.

It had the kind of saying sound
With which I was content
And never bothered very much
To wonder what it meant.

My father soon enlightened me
In manner most unkind.
What never troubled me before
Now troubled me behind.

My conscience hurt a day or two,
The rest of me a week.
That is the reason why I pause
And think before I speak.

Politician's Progress

He knew from hearsay life is hard,
But it remained for him to see;
So armored with a credit card
And university degree,
He galloped into history.

As yet not having made a stand,
He did not fear to take a fall.
If little went as he had planned,
At least it went, and after all
He had the nerve for it, and gall.

At last advancing to the take,
He learned the policy of give,
And bore the scar of each mistake
As brave men do who fight and live,
Grow old, and die conservative.

Miracle

Alone and waiting for the dawn to break
The old man on a narrow bed lay still
Forcing his thoughts through channels of his will
To some perspective that might ease the ache
Of human weakness, and an old mistake
He wore for penance foolishly until
He found forgiveness for the needless ill
That he and others suffered for his sake.

So gradually the miracle revealed
Itself to him and others near about
That they accepted healing, unaware
That in the process anything had healed
Beyond the faintest shadow of a doubt
Or rituals of a repeated prayer.

Hell Hounds

Now come the panting August Days
On stealthy pads of air
With shimmers tensed for sudden leap
And zeniths fixed at glare.

They lap at time with torrid tongues
And gnaw the green remains
Of grass, and leave a tawny shed
Like tufts from lions' manes.

We feel their hot and savage breath
So near they pass us by
While hunting down the fleecy clouds
Left mangled in the sky.

They cast behind a twilight look
That has a wilder glow
Than that of any wolf on earth
Or anything we know.

Summer Caravan

The spider's airy tent is down,
A rose lies shattered on the lawn,
And people waking in the town
Look out to find the summer gone.

Somewhere half way around the world
Barefooted children run to meet
The caravan with flags unfurled
Parading down some village street.

Brotherhood

Your principle denuded
Of every conscious act
Might be as starkly simple
As mine is in fact.

In timbers of our torture
The grain runs true and firm,

Resisting alike, unsplintered,
The driven nail and worm.

I feel your pain and thirsting,
And I would give you wine
And from your own cross lift you
Were I not nailed to mine.

Away

When Marilyn is gone from home
I see in passing by
A little mist of loneliness
Between the roof and sky.

The leaves have a dejected look
And hang down on the trees,
Whereas, when she is home they fly
Like banners in a breeze.

There is a difference somehow
On street and curb and lawn
Like after the parade has passed
And all the people gone.

Emily Dickinson

Sometimes I feel her presence
As in the nearest chair,
Vitality in essence
Invisible as air;
An eloquence of silence
Through which the minds can reach
Better communication
Than possible with speech.

Cycle

To the ruined garden
Where reigned the sacred rose
Now come the lowly petaled
That nobody knows,
That nobody cares for
And nobody sees
But grateful cattle
And perceptive bees.

The Lonely Ones

They look for vacant rooms in old hotels
Like hermit crabs that seek the cast-off shells
Along a beach,
And there in solitary scrutinize
A giddy world spinning before their eyes
And out of reach.

They plan to stay no longer than they must,
But for the most, the check-out time is DUST,
And then they go
With no one there to see them on the way,
Or keep some little token of their stay,
Or care . . . or even know.

Myself and I

I see you sitting there
Invisible in an empty chair,
My Youth of joy and sorrow,
And remember you lovingly
With a touch of horror.

I am what you became
Though we were and are the same
Through suffering and folly,
Triumphs and defeats,
The sad times and the jolly.

I remember the minor sinnings
And the thrill of new beginnings
Without an end to anything in sight.
The old glories are never the same
When seen in a different light.

Lady at High Noon

Her structure is triumphant in the flesh
Molded and curved on the enduring bone
The gears of her coordination mesh
And powered beauty moves upon its own.
The tawny hair, the blue, electric glance,
The rhythmicals of modulated speech,
The shapely hands pink-palmed by circumstance
Of having pleasant things in easy reach
Of ten demanding digits and a mood,
Earn dividend and bonus on her charm.
But in the attic of her solitude
A gnawed nerve frays and systems of alarm
Alert her to the unacknowledged fears
Of mouse-gray moments nibbling at her years.

Treadmill

He took the drink and left the job
For someone else to do instead;
And, having nowhere else to go,
Went home and took his wife to bed.

For her the novelty had worn
Too thin around the circumstance,
And so she gambled what she had
To win herself another chance.

She took the little that remained
Out of the nothing left behind
And fled without a change of heart
Or even making up her mind.

Guests

We look for the Expected,
And every nerve goes numb
Then the hour passes
And it has not come.

As for the Unexpected,
The mind somehow contrives
Proper accommodation
The moment it arrives.

Inevitable is final,
And though we have not spared
Ourselves in preparation,
It finds us unprepared.

Awesome Is the Passage

Light a holy candle,
Let its flicker shine
Casting grotesque shadows
Of your doubts and mine.

Light enough to see by
Is a thing to cherish;

Better walk with shadows
Than in the darkness perish.

Awesome is the passage
We must all pass through
And on steps uncertain
Make ourselves come true.

Blue

Blue is a chosen color
From Nature's royal dyes
With which Creation touches
The spaces of surprise
On morning's eastern border,
On hemlines of the west,
And lakes, and fragile treasure
Laid in a robin's nest.

Lost and Found

A mislaid pipe
When found smokes better.
Time mellows words
In an old love letter.

A familiar face
On a foreign street
Sets the heart drumming,
Hastens the feet.

The polar look
And frozen position
Melt in the light
Of warm recognition.

Hand touches hand,
Soul touches soul,
Restoring the missing
Parts to the whole.

A Man Remembered

Because he was familiar
To each of us as light at dawn,
Unthinking we accepted him
And smiled and spoke and hurried on.

But when a voice with greater range
Than ours was needed for a cause,
We called on him to speak for us
And trusted him for all he was.

We saw in him the better self
In each of us who fails and strives
And sinks into the final dark
To rise again in other lives.

No More the Buffalo

I am an old brave with reservations,
dreaming my medicine dream in a back yard.
I stare into space.
This is what I see:

No more the buffalo
graze high plains rolling
south beyond memory
and north beyond knowledge.
This is a cultured country now
with primal problems.
Man recognizes a problem;

it takes one to know one.
What have you done with vision,
you who mourn the end of old frontiers?
What have you done for freedom,
you who trample its symbol
and shout frustration in the streets?
WHERE WERE YOU WHEN OUR SCOUTS RETURNED
WITH MOON DUST ON THEIR MOCCASINS?

Views from a Window in Winter
Tree

From a window in my room
I see a peach tree in full bloom,
Which in the month of January
Seems delightfully contrary.

But there it is for real although
The wind is chill and threatens snow.
Potential peaches will be lost
For this defiance of the frost.

Mother Nature, hear my plea
For this audacious little tree
Guilty of no greater crime
Than flowering before its time!

Dead Bird

A fluff of crimson feathers on the lawn
And one bright singer missing from a bough;
The gift is broken and a joy is gone,
Wind sweeps away the empty wrapper now.

Window

A window is a narrow view
From which to watch the world about.
I think the wisest thing to do
Is simply turn me inside out.

The Four Winds

When the winds blows from the north
My solitary thoughts arise
On easy wings that cleave the air
To warmer lands and gentler skies.

When the wind blows from the south
I travel northward with the drift
To lonely tundras of the mind
And cold stars shining through a rift.

When the wind blows from the east
My way is westward with the rains
To where the mountains lift the sky
And tilt it over endless plains.

When the wind blows from the west
My words come like a lost bird's cry
Spontaneous with anguish
In zones of no reply.

Keep It Simple, Simon

If your eyes tire of the printed page,
Rest them in the leaves of trees
And read the promise of fruit to come.

If your ears ache from the traffics of commerce
And revelry, listen to the symphonies of wind and wave,
And relax to the hum of bees.

If polluted atmosphere cloys your living breath,
Breathe in the breath of the Spirit
That purifies body and soul.

If the weight of the pen or spade becomes too heavy,
Kneel on the earth on which you stand
And renew your strength with prayer.

If words become bitter on your lips,
Rinse your mouth with cool, spring water
And good taste will be restored unto you.

Be not confounded by paradox;
While the flesh applies cosmetics,
The soul bathes naked in Truth.

1879-1912

My mother was a prairie child
And all her features fair.
Her presence was a glint of sun,
A breath of morning air.
When Time return her to the dust,
Wild flowers blossomed there.

Requiem for a Friend

Tom is dead.
I am alive.
By clock the morning
Is poised at five.
By sun measure
It is four.
But time will trouble
Tom no more.
The shock has passed.
The tears are shed.
I am alive
And Tom is dead.
For the hand

That lost its touch
Let my hand
Reach out and clutch
Every lovely,
Living thing
Tom would be
Remembering
On a morning
Poised at five,
If I were dead
And Tom alive.
Grief is passing.
I rejoice
I can lend
His words my voice.
I loved his virtues,
Shared his flaws,
And can better
Serve his cause
With what time
That I can save
For memories
This side the grave.

Playing Dolls

The clutch of loving, careless hands
Too often tears the doll apart,
And bandages of reprimands
But little ease the childish heart.

The fragile remedies, too, fail:
A kiss, a wish upon a star,
And nothing seems of much avail
But Time's slow cautery . . . and scar.

Strange Species

There springs to life among expected flowers
A bloom from some obscure and dormant seed
Not listed in any catalogue of ours,
And therefore nameless and unpedigreed.

And so it is among the well scanned pages
Where famous poets at their best are shown
Creeps in some perennial of the ages
Whose simple listing reads: Author Unknown.

Somewhere

There is a place called Somewhere,
But not a chart to show
The latitude and longitude
For those who wish to go.

Himself, his own discoverer,
Must pay his own expense
And follow Faith, the only star
Beyond Experience.

The Fallen City

When one cannot distinguish
The bitter from the sweet
And doors are shut and silent
And Terror walks the street,
No help will be forthcoming,
No one will hear the cry
When sword and pen are futile
And time has come to die.
Say not one is forsaken,
Say not one is betrayed.
The living have surrendered;
The dead have fought and stayed.

Then

When the brook runs dry
and the dragonflies
come shimmering no more,
shadow skipping over ripples,
and the little frogs have departed
through the browning ferns,
I shall arise and go,
stepping to the measure
of a slow forgetting
while memory follows
ever farther behind
in long drifts of fallen days.

In Passing

In passing may the last thought in my mind
Be nothing shallow and yet not too deep
But something such as happy children find
In dreams that bring a smile into their sleep.

Afterword

A Memoir by Barbara Jo Brothers

In justice we must praise his strength
As we deplore his flaws.
Could we advance the flag so far
Though wounded, as he was?
                    —"Two Profiles of a Single Poet"

He dreamed of wings and was destined to crawl
A little while on an allotted span
Where roses are potential in each clod . . .
                    —"Say This Of Me"

His Forwarding Address

During the first Christmas season after my father's death in 1979, I invited my two nieces[1] from Texas, then fifteen and thirteen, to visit me in New Orleans.

Aware that the day—December 29, 1979—was their grandfather's birthday, I asked how they felt. Were they missing him?

The little one said, "No, not so much." Then she went on to say, "Aunt Barbara Jo, he prepared us for when he would die. He used to tell us about it. And besides, we are going to know right where to find him when we get to heaven."

"Oh," I said. "Where might that be?"

The little one, Dawn, continued in complete serious-
ness, "Well, when we first get to heaven, there will be a
train² station where we arrive. So the first thing we are sup-
posed to do when we get there is to get on the train and
ride it all the way to the end of the line. When we get off,
we will see a stage coach waiting for us there. We get in the
stage coach and ride it to the end of the line where there
will be another stage coach waiting for us. We take that
stage coach, too, and ride it all the way to the end of the
line—as far as it goes. When we get out, we will see some
horses tied there for us at the stage coach stop. From that
point, we have to go by horseback. After we have ridden all
day, we will begin to see a mountain range appearing in the
distance. We are supposed to ride toward the highest
mountain in that mountain range. When we get as far up
that mountain as we can go on horseback, we are to then
get off and climb to the top of the high ridge that will be
there above us. When we get to the top of the ridge we
should look down into the valley down below and we will
see a big circle of Indian teepees.

"Grandpa Lee will be down there with the Indians in
one of the teepees. He will be easy to find then, because he
will be a medicine man and everybody will know who he is.

"So all we have to do then is just go down the hill and
there is where he will be. And that is why we don't really
have to worry, Aunt Barbara Jo, because we know right
where we can find him."

This thirteen year-old child told me this in the same
spirit in which she would be telling me which streets to take
to get to her house in Bay City, Texas. For her, it was almost
as if he were only in Abilene or maybe El Paso. And there
was not a hint of a smile or any expression to suggest she
thought of this as anything but literal directions.

Blue Frontier

My father's practical skills in the grandfathering role

surpassed those of his parenting role. By the same token, whatever he may have lacked in fathering skills on the more tangible levels, in metaphysical mentoring he was peerless, even in my own childhood.

I remember how I used to feel lying on top of the wash shed with my father and my little sister on summer evenings, watching the sky for falling stars and flying saucers. If we looked long enough, we were sure to see one or the other. The heart of the Texas sky swept over us in all its possible acuteness; the Milky Way was usually almost bright enough to see your way home by. I grew up gazing into the galaxies. I do not mean to present this as a passive event when I speak of "watching." In fact, it seemed participatory. We fell back and forth into each other—we three and the stars.

"Blue Frontier" and "Summer Night" were born from such evenings. Infinity held great fascination for my father.

His Entry; His World

Life began for my father on December 29, 1908, in an area of Gonzales County, Texas, known as Big Hill. When Robert Lee, Jr., was three-and-a-half years old, his mother died while giving birth to his younger brother, Al, (named Alma, for her, and Brevard, for a brother lost to his father in his youth). Robert Lee's heart was broken; years later he recalled the dry misery he was feeling when he brushed away a piece of chewing gum some relative tried to offer by way of comfort as he left a room on the day of her funeral. In fact, his description of that time is sufficiently vivid that I carry the image in my mind of the day in mid-July, 1912, when those ministering to the dying woman were so preoccupied with the mother that they laid aside baby Al, taking him for dead. Aunt Mat, the black woman who served as nurse for generations of the children of our family, did take note and brought the infant into life with mouth-to-mouth resuscitation.

What the child Robert Lee seemed to do in response to this crushing loss was to turn to Nature for his mothering. His love of the land and fellow citizens of the land—the cardinal, the deer, the coyote, the wild plum blossom, and the "perceptive bees" (in "Cycle")—ran deep through his soul and out again, carrying the poems that appear in this volume.

He stayed on the ranch in his grandfather's large, two-story ranch house, playing in the sheltering limbs of the old oak trees and by the "meanders of the stream" (lines in "Embezzle the Sun"). A wild hedge rose grew along what much later—by the time I had entered the scene—became a fence line. Robert Lee, Jr., grew too, for the next couple of years, tended like a little king by the black ranch hands and servants, one of whom also had been responsible for saving his life in his infancy. He had an intolerance for milk, and the same Aunt Mat who had breathed life into his baby brother came up with a mixture of malt that his infant stomach could hold.

Aunt Mat—Martha Harper—was a pillar of security in his world. Years later, when I was a small child, our father would often take us on Sunday afternoons to the cemetery where his biological mother was buried, then to sit on Aunt Mat's front porch for the rest of the afternoon. Born just before the election of Abraham Lincoln, Martha Harper died at the age of 102 in the year of the election of John F. Kennedy. She was a grounding influence for my father—and a source more of wisdom than of comfort for him—throughout her long life. "Requiem for Aunt Martha 1861-1963" is written for her.

The child Robert Lee idolized his hell-raising, hard-drinking old grandfather, Lee M. Kokernot. On the day my father was born, Grandfather Kokernot gave his grandson the ranch on which I grew up, along with the cryptic curse/blessing: "He probably won't be any damn good, but the land will." The land that became our ranch was the "far pasture" in earlier days, located about seven miles from the ranch headquarters.

My father used to describe his utter fascination with his grandfather. He would sit at his knee to hear tales of adventure from the early days of Texas, of driving the cattle up the long trail to Kansas, of his service with Texas' Terry Rangers in the Civil War, of the vicissitudes that went with turning land and Longhorns into money in the mid to late 1800's in south central Texas. Soldiers and cowboys were very romantic figures to a little boy of four or five. Some of those stories gave rise to such poems as "Ballad of the Avengers," "A Grave in Boot Hill," and "Ear Marks and Brands." Because my father grew up on those stories, I grew up on his stories about those stories. To this day, my sister and I remember a garbled version of an Indian chant-song brought back from one of the trail drives along with a braided leather quirt ("The Quirt") from the Indian Territory that is now Oklahoma.

When Robert Lee was five and a half years old, his beloved grandfather died. Forced to move from the ranch which had cradled him since his mother's death, my father was left with a yearning he never lost—echoed in "From White Oblivions of Snow," "Long Remember," and even "The Hidden Harp." He always felt himself to be in a strange land after leaving the big ranch; it was the last place that felt like home.

My father built our house on the property's highest point—scrub oak and prolific clumps of prickly pear scattering out behind and to the north, the house facing east so that "the sun could come up like thunder outa China 'crost the bay." (Kipling, another poet he loved and often recited). The "bay" in our case was the rolling prairie on which our father was born. On that far eastern horizon was where the old ranch headquarters had been—the ranch my great grandfather had brought into being, birthed out of that era of the great trail drives to Kansas.

The land fulfilled its part of the old cattleman's prophecy. It nurtured us all through our various mixed blessings and was the gentle hand that brushed us toward prevailing in the face of all the less favorable portions of the legacy.

I returned to my birthplace recently, half-fearing I would feel like Walter de la Mare's "The Listeners" which my father had so often quoted when I was growing up. The lines were as haunting to me then in my childhood as they are now:

"Is there anybody there?" said the Traveler,
Knocking on the moonlit door . . .
. . . "Is there anybody there?" he said
But no one descended to the Traveler;
No head from the leaf-fringed sill
Leaned over and looked into his gray eyes
Where he stood perplexed and still . . .

In fact, the house was empty and did stare back—but not with that dread vacant stare. No, it was most curious—the hilltop converged into a single sentient entity as the dusk fell and I felt as if I might be back in the cozy kitchen of an elderly great aunt. I felt embraced and welcomed in the remembered hush that comes with the first edges of twilight.

In *fact*, I was standing on a sandy, weed-covered surface so ostensibly unreliable that my feet had already gone into that unconscious shifting dance that one is better off to adopt in most of the Texas countryside. The more pertinent fact is, if a person stands still for even a few minutes in that part of the country, some stinging, biting creature will begin an ascent of one's feet and fasten arthropodian "tooth and claw" at the first available point at the first available opportunity. And the Texas arthropod is often no mild beast. We grew up literally shaking our boots out every morning. One checked all surfaces—water glasses, bathtub, even pillowcases—for scorpions. My father's "Desert-Born," "Southwest," and "The Vulture" speak to the harsher aspects of the land.

However, this hilltop burst into bluebonnet bloom each spring and was a palpable rainbow that child me drifted through like Dickinson's inebriated bees—though I felt butterfly at the time.

We consciously celebrated all this. It was by no means taken for granted. My father rode home one day each year with the first Indian paintbrush of the season stuck in his hat band. I still have, tucked into one of his books of poems, a first bluebonnet from such a spring celebration long ago. In those days, he crushed these flowers carefully between the pages of Emily Dickinson's books. From this habit came his otherwise unpublished "Bluebonnet."

Today I took another look
At a bluebonnet pressed and dried
Between the pages of a book
That long ago I laid aside.

To me it seemed to bloom again
As in my hand I held it fast.
How strange such fragile links can chain
The present to the distant past.

Bluebonnets by the millions grow
Each year as far as one can see,
But there will be no more I know
That seem intended just for me.

In the days, one could step out on the porch and see the rain coming up from the river from the south; the rainbows threw themselves across the purple-blue prairie like paintings creating themselves. At night, the stars fell for us making their refraining trails, a nocturnal counterpart. None of this went unnoticed and I think, more and more, that it all settled in me in soul's garden where they still nurture me in some sweet way: a dewdrop here, a hunter's moon there, a fawn's soft startled stare, raindrops on the roof at night—the woodstove warm—the sour milk smell of butter being churned. Always the humming hills, cattle lowing, horse's willing wildness, rider ready, legs clenched against damp leather.

God knows, our life on the psychological/emotional

plane was often the opposite of idyllic. And yet, it was as if Nature Herself held out a protective net.

I know now that much of this was because my father saw it so—with his Dickinsonian bent, the natural landscape was reverently honored. It was not so much that he "wrote nature poems." It was rather as if he made frequent reports on the procession of Life as it was manifesting in all its various forms.

Our family cemetery is nestled near " . . . the little creek retiring / to a narrower bed . . ." ("Strange in the Sunset"), a few yards behind where the big house stood. A tall, granite obelisk built into the wall in the corner honors Lee Kokernot, the patriarch who built the world into which Robert Lee Brothers, Jr., was born. This is " . . . the ruined garden/ where reigned the sacred rose . . ." ("Cycles") to which he often brought my sister and me as children.

Our father is buried there. All three verses of "Reverie" are inscribed on his tombstone. The last verse reads

> When in the quiet interim I lie,
> All mortal things aside, needed no more
> Wrap me in prayer and face me to the sky
> And go with love, and gently close the door.

Robert Lee Brothers' tombstone stands beside the stone angel that has hovered over his mother's grave all these years:

> Now I watch, but soon I must
> Sleep beside you with the dust
> Still and dreamless on my eyes
> Wake me, Mother, when you rise.
> —"Beyond the Deep and Dreamless Sleep"

His footstone reads, "Home at Last." Coming generations will think it a religious reference. In truth, we meant it quite literally.

Papa is home at last.

His Soul's Companion: Emily Dickinson

We had a tree named Emily Dickinson.

On the way down to the river, right on the edge of the cleared pecan grove before the "river bottom" woods become dense and thick, stands a singularly beautiful acorn oak. Her limbs spread toward the sky with such grace and poetry, my father named her for his spiritual mother, Emily Dickinson, She was the prettiest tree in the pasture. We always said, "Hello, Emily," as we rode our horses past her; my father tipped his hat.

It is now clear to me how thoroughly Emily Dickinson permeated my childhood. My father wrote two poems for her—"To Emily Dickinson" (*The Hidden Harp*) and "Emily Dickinson" (*Late Harvest*)—and also quoted her on every applicable occasion, which made her almost a daily experience for me.

My father made a point of giving me, two or three years before his death, one of his treasured Emily Dickinson books, *The Final Harvest*. This particular book was my father's version of a diary. It had been precious to him. It had gone with him through all his adventures beginning with the point soon after he had begun his serious quest to declare himself "poet," to accept that state as the primary definition of his life. This was a topic we had discussed for years. Now he wanted me to have it; I think his giving it to me was a part of his beginning the letting go of life.

Opening it, one senses his dialogue with marked poems. There are many dates beside the poems—sometimes several dates by a particular one. He used it as a kind of cryptic projective diary. Very little is written except the dates. The major exception is on the fly leaf, on which he recorded the births of all three of my sister's children—his grandchildren:

My grandson
Joel Lee Paris—
Born November 30, 1962—
Child of the North Star

My granddaughter
Azilea Paris—
Born Oct. 20 - 64
Under The Hunter's Moon

My granddaughter
Dawn Janise Paris—
Born January 14, 1966—
Last quarter of moon of winter.

Mid-book appears the time he went to Tripoli for several months to visit his brother, Al. There are four unused Libyan, pre-Khadafi stamps between the pages. He notes the day he flew over Scotland, he notes a night in Spain. Later in the book, though earlier in terms of years, there is Mazatlan, the date and my initials. In 1963 I drove him across the north of Mexico in my little Volkswagen more or less on my way back to New Orleans to begin my professional life after graduate school. "Durango" was born on that trip.

As all these notes are beside specific poems, it is a sort of journal. For me, almost each poem Emily Dickinson wrote is like a little bell that calls out its own memories.

Until recently, when I had occasion to return to Emily Dickinson[3] for a thorough reading of her biography, letters, and poems, I had never consciously thought about her in my adulthood any more than one thinks consciously about one's grandmother. I inherited Dickinson like the Christians did Jesus. It was not that my father used to read Emily Dickinson to me and not that I even read her—he would recite whatever whole poem the given occasion suggested. He had committed to memory every well-known poem along with dozens of his own other favorites; I am not sure how many more. This was not some occasional let's-have-a-literary-evening. This was while riding the pasture with him, or on my very first arrival at college, probably my first day at school (all I remember for sure is the one he wrote for that occasion "First Day at School," but there were many). I see now that her theology very much influenced his which very much influenced mine. I think she has been a major origin of my own theological and philosophical leanings and my "closet" archetype for most of my life. She certainly was his.

Now, about half way through my life, what a surprise to discover how thoroughly the influence of Emily Dickinson, through her poetry, had come down through the years to me through the person and poetry of my father.

> *And on Steps Uncertain / Make Ourselves Come True*
> —"Awesome is the Passage"

So, perhaps, young Dawn is right about her Grandpa Lee as medicine man. He left me with the spirit of Emily Dickinson and the land woven into a whole piece and, thus, with a healing presence.

> His summons from Divinity
> Was briefly stated, "Come"
> And the immortal estimate
> Redeemed the mortal sum.
>
> His talent was requited then
> And he was blest indeed
> By simply sharing of himself
> In hemispheres of need.
> —"Two Profiles of a Single Poet"

May those who read the poetry of Robert Lee Brothers find themselves similarly blessed.

---

1 Azilea Paris Fehmel and Dawn Paris Bossley, now grown. Their mother—Robert Lee Brothers' younger daughter—Nancy Kaye Paris ("Proud Rider" and "For Two Girls in Their Teens") also bore his beloved grandson to whom *Threescore and Ten* is dedicated.

2 Trains were one of my father's favorite images: "Passenger," "Last Train Out," "Train Time."

3 As presented by Jean Houston in *Public Like a Frog*, 1993. Chicago, Illinois: Quest Books.

Acknowledgements

Poems from *Democracy of Dust* appeared in *Kaleidograph, Southern Literary Messenger, Spirit, Beat of Wings, Kansas City Poetry Magazine, Chipmunk, Reflections, Bright Mosaic, Covered Wagon, Scimitar and Song, Farming, The Lantern,* and *The Cattleman.*

Poems in *The Hidden Harp* were published earlier in *Kaleidograph, Poetry Society of Texas Yearbook, The Christian Science Monitor, The Gonzales Inquirer, The Staten Island Transcript, Stanza, Scimitar and Song, Quicksilver,* and *Writer's Magazine.*

Poems included in *Threescore and Ten* previously appeared in *Kaleidograph, The Kansas City Star, The Christian Science Monitor, Quicksilver, The Washington Star, The Denver Post, Poetry Society of Texas Yearbook, The Lyric,* and *The Gonzales Inquirer.*

A number of poems in *Late Harvest* appeared in *The Lyric*; one ("Time Reports 1863-1963") was published in *South and West.*

*   *   *   *   *

Several individuals deserve special thanks for their contributions to the publication of this volume. Bradley Farmer Avant of the Gonzales Chamber of Commerce published many of Brothers' poems during the two decades she served as associate editor of the Gonzales Inquirer. In numerous ways she has been instrumental in keeping intact the legacy of Robert Lee Brothers. Anne B. Lara and Tommye Corlew, staff members at Vanderbilt University, brought not only their skills but their Texas can-do spirit to the work of preparing the manuscript. Dr. Davis L. Ford of Austin, who knows good poetry when he sees it, believed in this publication and helped bring it about. Finally, we are grateful to Ed Eakin, whose vision of what is important sustains everything Eakin Press undertakes.